/Architectural Resources Cambridge · BraytonHughes Design Studios · CBT/Childs Bertman Tseckares · Francis Cauffm FXFOWLE Architects LLP ·
sler · Gerner Kronick + Valcarcel, Architects, PC · H. Hendy Associates · HLW International LLP HOK · Huntsman Architectural Group · Ken R. Harry
ociates, Inc. · LS3P ASSOCIATES LTD. · Margulies Perruzzi Architects McCarthy Nordburg · Mojo•Stumer · hitects Inc.
ins+Will · Rottet Studio – Architecture and Design · RTKL Associates Inc. · STAFFELBACK · Ted Moudis Ass rises · VOA
ociates Incorporated · Wolcott Architecture Interiors · Zimmer Gunsel Frasca Architects LLP · ARC/Architectu ghes Design
dios · CBT/Childs Bertman Tseckares · Francis Cauffm FXFOWLE Architects LLP · Gensler · Gerner Kronick + Valcarcel, Architects, PC · H. Hendy Associates · HLW
rnational LLP HOK · Huntsman Architectural Group · Ken R. Harry Associates, Inc. · LS3P ASSOCIATES LTD. · Margulies Perruzzi Architects McCarthy Nordburg ·
o•Stumer · NELSON · OWP/P · Partridge Architects Inc. · Perkins+Will · Rottet Studio – Architecture and Design · RTKL Associates Inc. · STAFFELBACK · Ted Moudis
ociates · Tobin + Parnes Design Enterprises · VOA Associates Incorporated · Wolcott Architecture Interiors · Zimmer Gunsel Frasca Architects LLP · ARC/Architectural
ources Cambridge · BraytonHughes Design Studios · CBT/Childs Bertman Tseckares · Francis Cauffm FXFOWLE Architects LLP · Gensler · Gerner Kronick +
arcel, Architects, PC · H. Hendy Associates · HLW International LLP HOK · Huntsman Architectural Group · Ken R. Harry Associates, Inc. · LS3P ASSOCIATES LTD.
rgulies Perruzzi Architects McCarthy Nordburg · Mojo•Stumer · NELSON · OWP/P · Partridge Architects Inc. · Perkins+Will · Rottet Studio – Architecture and Design
KL Associates Inc. · STAFFELBACK · Ted Moudis Associates · Tobin + Parnes Design Enterprises · VOA Associates Incorporated · Wolcott Architecture Interiors
mmer Gunsel Frasca Architects LLP ·ARC/Architectural Resources Cambridge · BraytonHughes Design Studios · CBT/Childs Bertman Tseckares · Francis Cauffm
OWLE Architects LLP · Gensler · Gerner Kronick + Valcarcel, Architects, PC · H. Hendy Associates · HLW International LLP HOK · Huntsman Architectural Group ·
R. Harry Associates, Inc. · LS3P ASSOCIATES LTD. · Margulies Perruzzi Architects McCarthy Nordburg · Mojo•Stumer · NELSON · OWP/P · Partridge Architects
· Perkins+Will · Rottet Studio – Architecture and Design · RTKL Associates Inc. · STAFFELBACK · Ted Moudis Associates · Tobin + Parnes Design Enterprises · VOA
ociates Incorporated · Wolcott Architecture Interiors · Zimmer Gunsel Frasca Architects LLP · ARC/Architectural Resources Cambridge · BraytonHughes Design Studios
T/Childs Bertman Tseckares · Francis Cauffm FXFOWLE Architects LLP ARC/Architectural Resources Cambridge · BraytonHughes Design Studios · CBT/Childs Bertman
ckares · Francis Cauffm FXFOWLE Architects LLP · Gensler · Gerner Kronick + Valcarcel, Architects, PC · H. Hendy Associates · HLW International LLP HOK · Huntsman
itectural Group · Ken R. Harry Associates, Inc. · LS3P ASSOCIATES LTD. · Margulies Perruzzi Architects McCarthy Nordburg · Mojo•Stumer · NELSON · OWP/P · Partridge
itects Inc. · Perkins+Will · Rottet Studio – Architecture and Design · RTKL Associates Inc. · STAFFELBACK · Ted Moudis Associates · Tobin + Parnes Design Enterprises · VOA
ociates Incorporated · Wolcott Architecture Interiors · Zimmer Gunsel Frasca Architects LLP · ARC/Architectural Resources Cambridge · BraytonHughes Design
dios · CBT/Childs Bertman Tseckares · Francis Cauffm FXFOWLE Architects LLP · Gensler · Gerner Kronick + Valcarcel, Architects, PC · H. Hendy Associates · HLW
rnational LLP HOK · Huntsman Architectural Group · Ken R. Harry Associates, Inc. · LS3P ASSOCIATES LTD. · Margulies Perruzzi Architects McCarthy Nordburg ·
o•Stumer · NELSON · OWP/P · Partridge Architects Inc. · Perkins+Will · Rottet Studio – Architecture and Design · RTKL Associates Inc. · STAFFELBACK · Ted Moudis
ociates · Tobin + Parnes Design Enterprises · VOA Associates Incorporated · Wolcott Architecture Interiors · Zimmer Gunsel Frasca Architects LLP · ARC/Architectural
ources Cambridge · BraytonHughes Design Studios · CBT/Childs Bertman Tseckares · Francis Cauffm FXFOWLE Architects LLP · Gensler · Gerner Kronick +
arcel, Architects, PC · H. Hendy Associates · HLW International LLP HOK · Huntsman Architectural Group · Ken R. Harry Associates, Inc. · LS3P ASSOCIATES
· Margulies Perruzzi Architects McCarthy Nordburg · Mojo•Stumer · NELSON · OWP/P · Partridge Architects Inc. · Perkins+Will · Rottet Studio –
itecture and Design · RTKL Associates Inc. · STAFFELBACK · Ted Moudis Associates · Tobin + Parnes Design Enterprises · VOA Associates Incorporated ·
cott Architecture Interiors · Zimmer Gunsel Frasca Architects LLP ·ARC/Architectural Resources Cambridge · BraytonHughes Design Studios · CBT/Childs
man Tseckares · Francis Cauffm FXFOWLE Architects LLP · Gensler · Gerner Kronick + Valcarcel, Architects, PC · H. Hendy Associates · HLW International
HOK · Huntsman Architectural Group · Ken R. Harry Associates, Inc. · LS3P ASSOCIATES LTD. · Margulies Perruzzi Architects McCarthy Nordburg ·
o•Stumer · NELSON · OWP/P · Partridge Architects Inc. · Perkins+Will · Rottet Studio – Architecture and Design · RTKL Associates Inc. · STAFFELBACK
d Moudis Associates · Tobin + Parnes Design Enterprises · VOA Associates Incorporated · Wolcott Architecture Interiors · Zimmer Gunsel Frasca Architects
· ARC/Architectural Resources Cambridge · BraytonHughes Design Studios · CBT/Childs Bertman Tseckares · Francis Cauffm FXFOWLE Architects LLP
ensler · Gerner Kronick + Valcarcel, Architects, PC · H. Hendy Associates · HLW International LLP HOK · Huntsman Architectural Group · Ken R. Harry
ociates, Inc. · LS3P ASSOCIATES LTD. · Margulies Perruzzi Architects McCarthy Nordburg · Mojo•Stumer · NELSON · OWP/P · Partridge Architects Inc. ·
kins+Will · Rottet Studio – Architecture and Design · RTKL Associates Inc. · STAFFELBACK · Ted Moudis Associates · Tobin + Parnes Design Enterprises · VOA
ociates Incorporated · Wolcott Architecture Interiors · Zimmer Gunsel Frasca Architects LLP · ARC/Architectural Resources Cambridge · BraytonHughes Design Studios
T/Childs Bertman Tseckares · Francis Cauffm FXFOWLE Architects LLP ARC/Architectural Resources Cambridge · BraytonHughes Design Studios · CBT/Childs Bertman
ckares · Francis Cauffm FXFOWLE Architects LLP · Gensler · Gerner Kronick + Valcarcel, Architects, PC · H. Hendy Associates · HLW International LLP HOK · Huntsman
itectural Group · Ken R. Harry Associates, Inc. · LS3P ASSOCIATES LTD. · Margulies Perruzzi Architects McCarthy Nordburg · Mojo•Stumer · NELSON · OWP/P · Partridge
itects Inc. · Perkins+Will · Rottet Studio – Architecture and Design · RTKL Associates Inc. · STAFFELBACK · Ted Moudis Associates · Tobin + Parnes Design Enterprises · VOA
ociates Incorporated · Wolcott Architecture Interiors · Zimmer Gunsel Frasca Architects LLP · ARC/Architectural Resources Cambridge · BraytonHughes Design
ources Cambridge · BraytonHughes Design Studios · CBT/Childs Bertman Tseckares · Francis Cauffm FXFOWLE Architects LLP · Gensler · Gerner Kronick +
arcel, Architects, PC · H. Hendy Associates · HLW International LLP HOK · Huntsman Architectural Group · Ken R. Harry Associates, Inc. · LS3P ASSOCIATES LTD.
rgulies Perruzzi Architects McCarthy Nordburg · Mojo•Stumer · NELSON · OWP/P · Partridge Architects Inc. · Perkins+Will · Rottet Studio – Architecture and Design
KL Associates Inc. · STAFFELBACK · Ted Moudis Associates · Tobin + Parnes Design Enterprises · VOA Associates Incorporated · Wolcott Architecture Interiors
mmer Gunsel Frasca Architects LLP ·ARC/Architectural Resources Cambridge · BraytonHughes Design Studios · CBT/Childs Bertman Tseckares · Francis Cauffm
OWLE Architects LLP · Gensler · Gerner Kronick + Valcarcel, Architects, PC · H. Hendy Associates · HLW International LLP HOK · Huntsman Architectural Group ·
R. Harry Associates, Inc. · LS3P ASSOCIATES LTD. · Margulies Perruzzi Architects McCarthy Nordburg · Mojo•Stumer · NELSON · OWP/P · Partridge Architects
· Perkins+Will · Rottet Studio – Architecture and Design · RTKL Associates Inc. · STAFFELBACK · Ted Moudis Associates · Tobin + Parnes Design Enterprises · VOA
ociates Incorporated · Wolcott Architecture Interiors · Zimmer Gunsel Frasca Architects LLP · ARC/Architectural Resources Cambridge · BraytonHughes Design Studios
T/Childs Bertman Tseckares · Francis Cauffm FXFOWLE Architects LLP ARC/Architectural Resources Cambridge · BraytonHughes Design Studios · CBT/Childs Bertman
ckares · Francis Cauffm FXFOWLE Architects LLP · Gensler · Gerner Kronick + Valcarcel, Architects, PC · H. Hendy Associates · HLW International LLP HOK · Huntsman
itectural Group · Ken R. Harry Associates, Inc. · LS3P ASSOCIATES LTD. · Margulies Perruzzi Architects McCarthy Nordburg · Mojo•Stumer · NELSON · OWP/P · Partridge
itects Inc. · Perkins+Will · Rottet Studio – Architecture and Design · RTKL Associates Inc. · STAFFELBACK · Ted Moudis Associates · Tobin + Parnes Design Enterprises · VOA
ociates Incorporated · Wolcott Architecture Interiors · Zimmer Gunsel Frasca Architects LLP · ARC/Architectural Resources Cambridge · BraytonHughes Design
dios · CBT/Childs Bertman Tseckares · Francis Cauffm FXFOWLE Architects LLP · Gensler · Gerner Kronick + Valcarcel, Architects, PC · H. Hendy Associates · HLW
rnational LLP HOK · Huntsman Architectural Group · Ken R. Harry Associates, Inc. · LS3P ASSOCIATES LTD. · Margulies Perruzzi Architects McCarthy Nordburg ·
o•Stumer · NELSON · OWP/P · Partridge Architects Inc. · Perkins+Will · Rottet Studio – Architecture and Design · RTKL Associates Inc. · STAFFELBACK · Ted Moudis
ociates · Tobin + Parnes Design Enterprises · VOA Associates Incorporated · Wolcott Architecture Interiors · Zimmer Gunsel Frasca Architects LLP · ARC/Architectural
ources Cambridge · BraytonHughes Design Studios · CBT/Childs Bertman Tseckares · Francis Cauffm FXFOWLE Architects LLP · Gensler · Gerner Kronick +
arcel, Architects, PC · H. Hendy Associates · HLW International LLP HOK · Huntsman Architectural Group · Ken R. Harry Associates, Inc. · LS3P ASSOCIATES LTD.
rgulies Perruzzi Architects McCarthy Nordburg · Mojo•Stumer · NELSON · OWP/P · Partridge Architects Inc. · Perkins+Will · Rottet Studio – Architecture and Design
KL Associates Inc. · STAFFELBACK · Ted Moudis Associates · Tobin + Parnes Design Enterprises · VOA Associates Incorporated · Wolcott Architecture Interiors
mmer Gunsel Frasca Architects LLP · ARC/Architectural Resources Cambridge · BraytonHughes Design Studios · CBT/Childs Bertman Tseckares · Francis Cauffm

ARC/Architectural Resources Cambridge · BraytonHughes Design Studios · CBT/Childs Bertman Tseckares · Francis Cauffm FXFOWLE Architects LL
Gensler · Gerner Kronick + Valcarcel, Architects, PC · H. Hendy Associates · HLW International LLP HOK · Huntsman Architectural Group · Ken R. H
Associates, Inc. · LS3P ASSOCIATES LTD. · Margulies Perruzzi Architects McCarthy Nordburg · Mojo•Stumer · NELSON · OWP/P · Partridge Architects Ir
Perkins+Will · Rottet Studio – Architecture and Design · RTKL Associates Inc. · STAFFELBACK · Ted Moudis Associates · Tobin + Parnes Design Enterprises · V
Associates Incorporated · Wolcott Architecture Interiors · Zimmer Gunsel Frasca Architects LLP · ARC/Architectural Resources Cambridge · BraytonHughes De
Studios · CBT/Childs Bertman Tseckares · Francis Cauffm FXFOWLE Architects LLP · Gensler · Gerner Kronick + Valcarcel, Architects, PC · H. Hendy Associates · H
International LLP HOK · Huntsman Architectural Group · Ken R. Harry Associates, Inc. · LS3P ASSOCIATES LTD. · Margulies Perruzzi Architects McCarthy Nordbu
Mojo•Stumer · NELSON · OWP/P · Partridge Architects Inc. · Perkins+Will · Rottet Studio – Architecture and Design · RTKL Associates Inc. · STAFFELBACK · Ted Mo
Associates · Tobin + Parnes Design Enterprises · VOA Associates Incorporated · Wolcott Architecture Interiors · Zimmer Gunsel Frasca Architects LLP · ARC/Architect
Resources Cambridge · BraytonHughes Design Studios · CBT/Childs Bertman Tseckares · Francis Cauffm FXFOWLE Architects LLP · Gensler · Gerner Kroni
Valcarcel, Architects, PC · H. Hendy Associates · HLW International LLP HOK · Huntsman Architectural Group · Ken R. Harry Associates, Inc. · LS3P ASSOCIATES
· Margulies Perruzzi Architects McCarthy Nordburg · Mojo•Stumer · NELSON · OWP/P · Partridge Architects Inc. · Perkins+Will · Rottet Studio – Architecture and De
· RTKL Associates Inc. · STAFFELBACK · Ted Moudis Associates · Tobin + Parnes Design Enterprises · VOA Associates Incorporated · Wolcott Architecture Inte
· Zimmer Gunsel Frasca Architects LLP ·ARC/Architectural Resources Cambridge · BraytonHughes Design Studios · CBT/Childs Bertman Tseckares · Francis Cau
FXFOWLE Architects LLP · Gensler · Gerner Kronick + Valcarcel, Architects, PC · H. Hendy Associates · HLW International LLP HOK · Huntsman Architectural Gro
Ken R. Harry Associates, Inc. · LS3P ASSOCIATES LTD. · Margulies Perruzzi Architects McCarthy Nordburg · Mojo•Stumer · NELSON · OWP/P · Partridge Archit
Inc. · Perkins+Will · Rottet Studio – Architecture and Design · RTKL Associates Inc. · STAFFELBACK · Ted Moudis Associates · Tobin + Parnes Design Enterprises · V
Associates Incorporated · Wolcott Architecture Interiors · Zimmer Gunsel Frasca Architects LLP · ARC/Architectural Resources Cambridge · BraytonHughes Design Stu
· CBT/Childs Bertman Tseckares · Francis Cauffm FXFOWLE Architects LLP ARC/Architectural Resources Cambridge · BraytonHughes Design Studios · CBT/Childs Bert
Tseckares · Francis Cauffm FXFOWLE Architects LLP · Gensler · Gerner Kronick + Valcarcel, Architects, PC · H. Hendy Associates · HLW International LLP HOK · Hunts
Architectural Group · Ken R. Harry Associates, Inc. · LS3P ASSOCIATES LTD. · Margulies Perruzzi Architects McCarthy Nordburg · Mojo•Stumer · NELSON · OWP/P · Partr
Architects Inc. · Perkins+Will · Rottet Studio – Architecture and Design · RTKL Associates Inc. · STAFFELBACK · Ted Moudis Associates · Tobin + Parnes Design Enterprises · V
Associates Incorporated · Wolcott Architecture Interiors · Zimmer Gunsel Frasca Architects LLP · ARC/Architectural Resources Cambridge · BraytonHughes De
Studios · CBT/Childs Bertman Tseckares · Francis Cauffm FXFOWLE Architects LLP · Gensler · Gerner Kronick + Valcarcel, Architects, PC · H. Hendy Associates · H
International LLP HOK · Huntsman Architectural Group · Ken R. Harry Associates, Inc. · LS3P ASSOCIATES LTD. · Margulies Perruzzi Architects McCarthy Nordbu
Mojo•Stumer · NELSON · OWP/P · Partridge Architects Inc. · Perkins+Will · Rottet Studio – Architecture and Design · RTKL Associates Inc. · STAFFELBACK · Ted Mo
Associates · Tobin + Parnes Design Enterprises · VOA Associates Incorporated · Wolcott Architecture Interiors · Zimmer Gunsel Frasca Architects LLP · ARC/Architec
Resources Cambridge · BraytonHughes Design Studios · CBT/Childs Bertman Tseckares · Francis Cauffm FXFOWLE Architects LLP · Gensler · Gerner Kroni
Valcarcel, Architects, PC · H. Hendy Associates · HLW International LLP HOK · Huntsman Architectural Group · Ken R. Harry Associates, Inc. · LS3P ASSOCIA
LTD. · Margulies Perruzzi Architects McCarthy Nordburg · Mojo•Stumer · NELSON · OWP/P · Partridge Architects Inc. · Perkins+Will · Rottet Stuc
Architecture and Design · RTKL Associates Inc. · STAFFELBACK · Ted Moudis Associates · Tobin + Parnes Design Enterprises · VOA Associates Incorporat
Wolcott Architecture Interiors · Zimmer Gunsel Frasca Architects LLP ·ARC/Architectural Resources Cambridge · BraytonHughes Design Studios · CBT/C
Bertman Tseckares · Francis Cauffm FXFOWLE Architects LLP · Gensler · Gerner Kronick + Valcarcel, Architects, PC · H. Hendy Associates · HLW Internati
LLP HOK · Huntsman Architectural Group · Ken R. Harry Associates, Inc. · LS3P ASSOCIATES LTD. · Margulies Perruzzi Architects McCarthy Nordbu
Mojo•Stumer · NELSON · OWP/P · Partridge Architects Inc. · Perkins+Will · Rottet Studio – Architecture and Design · RTKL Associates Inc. · STAFFELB
· Ted Moudis Associates · Tobin + Parnes Design Enterprises · VOA Associates Incorporated · Wolcott Architecture Interiors · Zimmer Gunsel Frasca Archit
LLP ·ARC/Architectural Resources Cambridge · BraytonHughes Design Studios · CBT/Childs Bertman Tseckares · Francis Cauffm FXFOWLE Architects
· Gensler · Gerner Kronick + Valcarcel, Architects, PC · H. Hendy Associates · HLW International LLP HOK · Huntsman Architectural Group · Ken R. H
Associates, Inc. · LS3P ASSOCIATES LTD. · Margulies Perruzzi Architects McCarthy Nordburg · Mojo•Stumer · NELSON · OWP/P · Partridge Architects Ir
Perkins+Will · Rottet Studio – Architecture and Design · RTKL Associates Inc. · STAFFELBACK · Ted Moudis Associates · Tobin + Parnes Design Enterprises · V
Associates Incorporated · Wolcott Architecture Interiors · Zimmer Gunsel Frasca Architects LLP · ARC/Architectural Resources Cambridge · BraytonHughes Design Stu
· CBT/Childs Bertman Tseckares · Francis Cauffm FXFOWLE Architects LLP ARC/Architectural Resources Cambridge · BraytonHughes Design Studios · CBT/Childs Bert
Tseckares · Francis Cauffm FXFOWLE Architects LLP · Gensler · Gerner Kronick + Valcarcel, Architects, PC · H. Hendy Associates · HLW International LLP HOK · Hunts
Architectural Group · Ken R. Harry Associates, Inc. · LS3P ASSOCIATES LTD. · Margulies Perruzzi Architects McCarthy Nordburg · Mojo•Stumer · NELSON · OWP/P · Partr
Architects Inc. · Perkins+Will · Rottet Studio – Architecture and Design · RTKL Associates Inc. · STAFFELBACK · Ted Moudis Associates · Tobin + Parnes Design Enterprises · V
Associates Incorporated · Wolcott Architecture Interiors · Zimmer Gunsel Frasca Architects LLP · ARC/Architectural Resources Cambridge · BraytonHughes De
Resources Cambridge · BraytonHughes Design Studios · CBT/Childs Bertman Tseckares · Francis Cauffm FXFOWLE Architects LLP · Gensler · Gerner Kroni
Valcarcel, Architects, PC · H. Hendy Associates · HLW International LLP HOK · Huntsman Architectural Group · Ken R. Harry Associates, Inc. · LS3P ASSOCIATES
· Margulies Perruzzi Architects McCarthy Nordburg · Mojo•Stumer · NELSON · OWP/P · Partridge Architects Inc. · Perkins+Will · Rottet Studio – Architecture and De
· RTKL Associates Inc. · STAFFELBACK · Ted Moudis Associates · Tobin + Parnes Design Enterprises · VOA Associates Incorporated · Wolcott Architecture Inte
· Zimmer Gunsel Frasca Architects LLP ·ARC/Architectural Resources Cambridge · BraytonHughes Design Studios · CBT/Childs Bertman Tseckares · Francis Cau
FXFOWLE Architects LLP · Gensler · Gerner Kronick + Valcarcel, Architects, PC · H. Hendy Associates · HLW International LLP HOK · Huntsman Architectural Gro
Ken R. Harry Associates, Inc. · LS3P ASSOCIATES LTD. · Margulies Perruzzi Architects McCarthy Nordburg · Mojo•Stumer · NELSON · OWP/P · Partridge Archit
Inc. · Perkins+Will · Rottet Studio – Architecture and Design · RTKL Associates Inc. · STAFFELBACK · Ted Moudis Associates · Tobin + Parnes Design Enterprises · V
Associates Incorporated · Wolcott Architecture Interiors · Zimmer Gunsel Frasca Architects LLP · ARC/Architectural Resources Cambridge · BraytonHughes Design Stu
· CBT/Childs Bertman Tseckares · Francis Cauffm FXFOWLE Architects LLP ARC/Architectural Resources Cambridge · BraytonHughes Design Studios · CBT/Childs Bert
Tseckares · Francis Cauffm FXFOWLE Architects LLP · Gensler · Gerner Kronick + Valcarcel, Architects, PC · H. Hendy Associates · HLW International LLP HOK · Hunts
Architectural Group · Ken R. Harry Associates, Inc. · LS3P ASSOCIATES LTD. · Margulies Perruzzi Architects McCarthy Nordburg · Mojo•Stumer · NELSON · OWP/P · Partr
Architects Inc. · Perkins+Will · Rottet Studio – Architecture and Design · RTKL Associates Inc. · STAFFELBACK · Ted Moudis Associates · Tobin + Parnes Design Enterprises · V
Associates Incorporated · Wolcott Architecture Interiors · Zimmer Gunsel Frasca Architects LLP · ARC/Architectural Resources Cambridge · BraytonHughes De
Studios · CBT/Childs Bertman Tseckares · Francis Cauffm FXFOWLE Architects LLP · Gensler · Gerner Kronick + Valcarcel, Architects, PC · H. Hendy Associates · H
International LLP HOK · Huntsman Architectural Group · Ken R. Harry Associates, Inc. · LS3P ASSOCIATES LTD. · Margulies Perruzzi Architects McCarthy Nordbu
Mojo•Stumer · NELSON · OWP/P · Partridge Architects Inc. · Perkins+Will · Rottet Studio – Architecture and Design · RTKL Associates Inc. · STAFFELBACK · Ted Mo
Associates · Tobin + Parnes Design Enterprises · VOA Associates Incorporated · Wolcott Architecture Interiors · Zimmer Gunsel Frasca Architects LLP · ARC/Architec
Resources Cambridge · BraytonHughes Design Studios · CBT/Childs Bertman Tseckares · Francis Cauffm FXFOWLE Architects LLP · Gensler · Gerner Kroni
Valcarcel, Architects, PC · H. Hendy Associates · HLW International LLP HOK · Huntsman Architectural Group · Ken R. Harry Associates, Inc. · LS3P ASSOCIATES
· Margulies Perruzzi Architects McCarthy Nordburg · Mojo•Stumer · NELSON · OWP/P · Partridge Architects Inc. · Perkins+Will · Rottet Studio – Architecture and De
· RTKL Associates Inc. · STAFFELBACK · Ted Moudis Associates · Tobin + Parnes Design Enterprises · VOA Associates Incorporated · Wolcott Architecture Inte
· Zimmer Gunsel Frasca Architects LLP ·ARC/Architectural Resources Cambridge · BraytonHughes Design Studios · CBT/Childs Bertman Tseckares · Francis Ca

Corporate Interiors

No. 9

Corporate Interiors

No. 9

Roger Yee

Visual Reference Publications Inc., New York

Opposite: RMB Capital Management LLC. **Design firm:** VOA. **Photography:** Nick Merrick/Hedrich Blessing.

Corporate Interiors No. 9

Visual Reference Publications, Inc.
302 Fifth Avenue • New York, NY 10001
Tel: 212.279.7000 • Fax: 212.279.7014 • Fax: 212.279.7014

www.visualreference.com

GROUP PUBLISHER	Larry Fuersich larry@visualreference.com
PUBLISHER	Bill Ash bill@visualreference.com
EDITORIAL DIRECTOR	Roger Yee yeerh@aol.com
CREATIVE ART DIRECTOR	Veronika Levin veronika@visualreference.com
ASSISTANT ART DIRECTORS	Candice Chu candice@visualreference.com
	Martina Parisi martina@visualreference.com
PRODUCTION MANAGER	John Hogan johnhvrp@yahoo.com
CIRCULATION MANAGER	Amy-Mei Li amy@visualreference.com
MARKETING COORDINATOR	Nika Chopra nika@visualreference.com
CONTROLLER	Angie Goulimis angie@visualreference.com

ISBN: 978-1-58471-159-9

Distributors to the trade in the United States and Canada
Innovative Logistics
575 Prospect Street
Lakewood, NJ 08701
732.363.5679

Distributors outside the United States and Canada
HarperCollins International
10 East 53rd Street
New York, NY 10022-5299

Exclusive distributor in China
Beijing Designerbooks Co., Ltd.
B-0619, No.2 Building, Dacheng International Center
78 East 4th Ring Middle Road
Chaoyang District, Beijing 100022, P.R. China
Tel: 0086(010)5962-6195 Fax: 0086(010)5962-6193
E-mail: info@designerbooks.net www.designerbooks.net

Printed and bound in China

Book Design: Veronika Levin

The paper on which this book is printed contains recycled content to support a sustainable world.

RIOLA

People say you should never sit on a good idea.
We tend to disagree.

dauphin
HumanDesign®

800.631.1186 · www.dauphin.com

Contents

HALCON:1811 2ND AVENUE NW   STEWARTVILLE, MINNESOTA 55976   TEL 507.533.4235

ATTACHÉ

HALCON

HALCONCORP.COM

LUNA

hum
Minds at Work.™

Furniture has always been
made to fit our bodies.
Why hasn't it been designed
to fit our minds?

www.humoffice.com

Kimball®Office

CROSSVILLE
ELEVATE YOUR SPACE

Product featured: Recycled Glass

www.crossvilleinc.com

What Does Your Office Say About You?

Where you work may increasingly depend on what—and whom—your work involves at a given hour, day or month, transforming office design as never before

More astonishing to Americans watching the Beijing Olympics in the summer of 2008 than swimmer Michael Phelps or China's fantastic architecture and world-class athletes was the Middle Kingdom's swift rise as an economic power. Here was a totalitarian state that seemed intent on destroying itself in Mao Zedong's Cultural Revolution of the 1960s, where market forces began shaping its economy under Deng Xiaoping just two decades ago, sitting atop a trade surplus with the United States that reached $243 billion in 2005. Not content to manufacture just toys, clothing, home appliances and other labor-intensive products, today's China builds iPhones for Apple.

The impact of the new world order, where the developing world is targeting the markets, industries and jobs of industrialized nations with growing accuracy, is being felt in the office environment. Not only is the outsourcing of jobs reaching ever higher levels of education, knowledge and skill—Wall Street giants like Goldman Sachs, Morgan Stanley and Citibank are now "offshoring" work done by research associates and junior bankers paid in the low to mid-six figures to India—but pressure is mounting for Americans to justify the jobs they still have. Paradoxically, the new pragmatism is actually creating a workplace better suited to work and workers than ever before.

Corporate America is dropping the traditional trappings of hierarchy in favor of a people-, process- and technology-driven environment where design creates multiple work venues, providing options for differing job tasks, project teams and times in the workday. That's not to say CEOs are being denied their corner suites. However, more workers are housed in workplace environments that reflect what they do and how they do it rather than where they stand in the organization.

This increasingly means an open, well-equipped, healthy and attractive office for all employees. Private offices are fewer in number, smaller in size and often enclosed in glass, while compact open workstations have low partitions between occupants, promoting accessibility along with the transmission of daylight and outdoor views deep inside their buildings. Formal and informal meeting rooms, team rooms, coffee bars, touchdown stations, cafeterias, lounges and the like encourage collaboration and give people optional and officially sanctioned places to work besides their desks. Advanced office and building technologies support virtually any task wherever people are. Ergonomic furnishings take their place alongside building products and interior finishes that give workers the advantages of sustainable design, energy and water conservation, and quality indoor air and illumination.

As readers of *Corporate Interiors No. 9* will also notice, the new office settings are physically attractive even when they aren't lavish. In the intensely visual world of the Internet, GPSs and DVDs, corporations and institutions are recognizing that well-designed workplaces can actually raise worker productivity and morale. The recently completed projects by leading architects and interior designers that appear on the following pages reflect this realization. They're demonstrating that good design translates into good business in corporate centers as far flung as Houston, Paris and Shanghai.

Roger Yee

Editor

Elements Conference
Elements Conference
Elements Conference
Elements Conference

VERSTEEL

ELEMENTS CONFERENCE®
WITH ENTOURAGE™ AND SIMON®

FUNCTIONAL A TABLE FOR EVERY SPACE.
A multitude of top shapes and sizes with complementary round, square or arced bases provide you with a perfect choice for conference needs.
ENDURING ENGINEERED AND BUILT TO VERSTEEL STANDARDS.
Powder coated steel frames and panels will provide unparalleled product longevity.
COHESIVE INTEGRATES WITH OTHER VERSTEEL PRODUCTS.
Combine with Entourage pieces and unique Versteel seating options to specify a complete conference area.

VERSTEEL ®

CALL **800 876 2120** OR VISIT **versteel.com**

If you're going to leave a footprint...

leave it here.

TAMBIENT™

Minimize your carbon footprint.

Task AND ambient lighting from a single T5 lamp.
0.6 watts per square foot.

green in any color.
www.Tambient.com

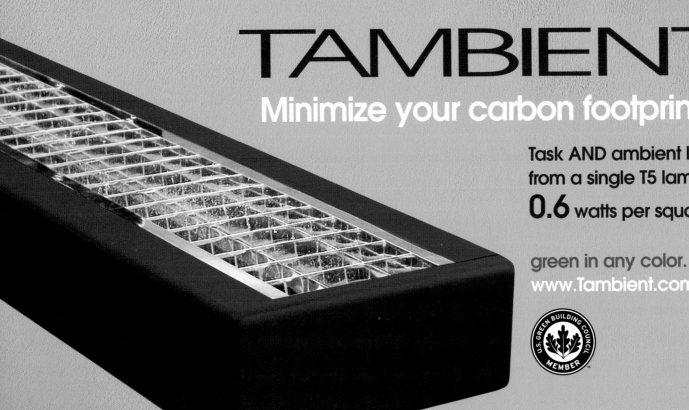

ARC/Architectural Resources Cambridge

ARC/Architectural Resources Cambridge

Genzyme Corporation
Science Center
Framingham, Massachusetts

Right: Main street facade and visitors' entry.

Bottom left: Reception and lobby.

Bottom right: Double-height conference room.

Opposite: Six-story atrium.

Photography: John Horner.

Visitors to Genzyme Corporation's new Science Center, in Framingham, Massachusetts, designed by ARC/Architectural Resources Cambridge, can easily understand why virtually anyone would be delighted to work there. Consolidating some 350 researchers and staff members who once occupied multiple locations, the six-story, 177,000-square-foot Science Center is imaginatively configured to enhance relationships, collaboration and flow of information among 16 different Genzyme research groups. This spacious and airy structure is a major milestone for this leading biotechnology company, founded in 1981 to make a major positive impact on the lives of people with debilitating diseases. Complex as its organization is—comprised of flexible laboratories and support spaces, private offices, conference rooms, write-up areas, reading lounges/ periodical library, coffee bars and cafeteria/servery— wayfinding within its largely glass-sheathed exterior is surprisingly uncomplicated, thanks to the luminous, atrium at the building's core. The six-story atrium, featuring monumental

ARC/Architectural Resources Cambridge

elevations, generous skylights and a unique, interweaving staircase, embodies the Science Center's pursuit of open space and natural lighting, one of numerous characteristics that distinguish it from typical laboratories. For example, all write-up stations have been moved from laboratory areas to the building perimeter and separated by glass walls and sliding doors to not only improve safety for laboratory personnel but also provide them with natural light. In addition, light shelves and glass walls are used to let natural light penetrate into the building core where the laboratories reside. The laboratories themselves are fitted out as large, open-plan spaces

with minimal customization to facilitate re-assignment and promote communication between different groups sharing common laboratory spaces. Equally important is the design's commitment to the versatile, attractive and sustainable environment, which recently earned the building the coveted LEED Gold Certification from the U.S. Green Building Council. The interior's predominately white color scheme, accented by natural tones (such as beech wood, slate and cork) and industrial finishes (such as glass, aluminum and blue aniline-dyed wood), combines with stylish contemporary furnishings to make offices, meeting spaces and lounges contrast

favorably with state-of-the-art laboratories and scientific equipment. This sophisticated approach recognizes the long, intense hours researchers devote to their work, as well as the value of chance encounters and social interaction among colleagues. Commenting on the award-winning facility's qualities, Rich Gregory, senior vice president and head of research at Genzyme Corporation, declares, "As our center of research activities, this building is the focal point of our Framingham R&D campus...[It] has had a very positive effect on morale with people enjoying the open spaces and new possibilities for casual, unplanned meetings."

Above: Write-up stations adjacent to labs.

Right: Top floor cafeteria with servery beyond.

Below: Typical laboratory.

Opposite bottom left: Coffee bar off of the central atrium.

Opposite bottom right: Periodical library.

ARC/Architectural Resources Cambridge

ARC/Architectural Resources Cambridge
Cambridge, Massachusetts

Every architecture firm knows how challenging the design of its own space can be. To develop a new, one-floor, 17,705-square-foot studio/office fit-out for 60 staff members, ARC/Architectural Resources Cambridge empowered a small committee that not only reviewed the project design and maintained the schedule, but also received input from its

talented designers by holding, presentations at key moments to gain consensus. The firm's aggressive approach to the project—streamlining the design process within its own office and integrating a construction management team into the project at the onset—proved critical in minimizing time and cost. As a result, the project came in on time and budget, provid-

ing a clean, contemporary facility with open studios, interior offices, conference rooms, and support space that exemplified the firm's team-based approach to practice. Key to the project's success is a spatial organization that has expanded the building core to include required service and storage, placed major circulation around the core, and

positioned glass-enclosed private offices in interior spaces. Open studios along the building perimeter enable everyone to enjoy access to daylight as well as unobstructed views of the Boston skyline. Observes Henry S. Reeder, FAIA, chairman of ARC, "The project has met every expectation of both the firm and our clients."

Below: Reception area and main conference room.

Opposite right: Open studios and glass-enclosed offices.

Opposite bottom right: "Design Review" pin-up area.

Photography: Robert Benson.

ARC/Architectural Resources Cambridge

A Virtual Software Company
Cambridge, Massachusetts

Software developers know all too well the quirky ways of their calling. Brilliant moments of creativity are routinely accompanied by exacting hours of concentrated work to produce significant new products. However, this hasn't prevented a virtual software company in Cambridge, Massachusetts, which offers a cutting-edge approach to personal computing and server utilization, from creating a more enjoyable and inspiring environment for its employees. In fact, the company recently completed its new, three-floor, 53,000-square-foot office in Cambridge, Massachusetts

for 240 people, designed by ARC/Architectural Resources Cambridge, to support a culture of teamwork in the new workplace. Besides providing general office space, data laboratories, conference rooms, and training rooms, the new facility offers a multi-purpose room, staff lounge and kitchen, and other amenities that reflect the company's distinctive atmosphere and dedicated work ethic. Of course, the data laboratories received specific security arrangements and specialized power and cooling provisions. Overall, however, the design represents a transparent and open workplace with quiet

breakout spaces for concentration offset by active spaces for downtime relaxation and socializing. Engulfed in bright colors, natural wood finishes, interior glass walls, textured and playful fabrics, and informal and flexible contemporary furnishings, employees are discovering that they can have "fun" while pursuing their passion for innovation and excellence in technology.

Top: Conference room with smaller meeting room and lounge.

Above: Reception.

Right: Multi-purpose room.

Photography: Studio of Warren Patterson.

BraytonHughes Design Studios

Architecture • Planning • Interior Design

BraytonHughes Design Studios

Montgomery & Co.
San Francsico, California

In its vision of the future, Montgomery & Co., a prominent investment bank founded in 1986, has emphasized its ability to be the top performer in its industry, remaining open and accessible in its work and staying on the forefront of technology. Putting words into action, Montgomery recently moved into a new, two-story, 13,600-square-foot executive and administrative office, designed by BraytonHughes Design Studios, placing employees on the top two floors of San Francisco's Two Embarcadero Center. It's clear that the stylish, minimal spaces constituting this contemporary facility—including the perimeter executive offices and support areas with conference rooms on the upper floor overlooking San Francisco Bay, and the reception area, adjacent boardroom and meeting rooms, staff offices, trading desks and support spaces on the lower floor—demanded intensive effort and yielded exceptional rewards. The design represents an inspired adaptation of the building's pinnacle, where the floor plate reduces to only a corridor and two offices in width, to give all occupants quality workspaces infused with daylight and panoramic views. From the floor-to-ceiling glass curtainwall that provides the aesthetic vocabulary, the design team has developed a complementary

Top left: Private office.
Above: Interior stair.
Left: Conference room.
Opposite: Boardroom.
Photography: John Sutton.

BraytonHughes Design Studios

system of glass partitions and sliding doors with polished aluminum structural frames so thin that the glass virtually disappears, promoting full transparency throughout each floor. These shimmering planes are accompanied by a minimal palette of pale white limestone, desk tops of curly maple dyed to produce a cloud-like appearance, translucent blue glass, polished stainless steel and aluminum, and white work surfaces. Their floating, ethereal quality is reprised by fabrics and carpeting in pale hues, clean, contemporary furniture, and lighting fixtures chosen for their Spartan elegance. Unseen by the typical observer, however, are the ingenious design and engineering that make this high-tech aerie possible. Because the upper floor was not originally designed for tenant occupancy, the two floors are connected by a new

glass-enclosed elevator and interior stair of "floating" limestone treads with glass risers. In addition, potential vibration and acoustical problems stemming from the existing mechanical system on the floor above required a structural support system that is cantilevered off the floor to support the walls and sliding doors without touching the deck above. Of course, what truly matters to Montgomery's employees is that their calm, reflective and minimally elegant new office will help them stay at the top of their game.

Right: Entrance to boardroom.
Below: Reception.
Opposite: Private office.

BraytonHughes Design Studios

Private Equity Firm
San Francisco, California

Right: Reception.
Below right: Conference room.
Opposite: Small conference room.
Photography: John Sutton.

A stratospheric view of San Francisco provides a breathtaking backdrop for employees of a private equity firm in their new, 12,000-square-foot executive office, designed by BraytonHughes Design Studios, on one of the top floors of One Maritime Plaza, in the heart of the city's financial district. In fact, the space that houses the reception area, boardroom, two medium-size conference rooms, private offices, administrative workstations, kitchen, storage and copy areas offers spectacular views from every window. Capturing these views while providing privacy, comfort and style is what makes this contemporary workplace so outstanding. For example, the interior construction of wood, glass and etched glass walls, sliding doors and rotating screens creates a consistent rhythm of open and closed modules along the perimeter that keeps the city in sight even when privacy is required. The administrative workstations lining the interior walls of perimeter spaces stay low to avoid obstructing the views while providing work surface and storage, and support functions and file space cluster around the building core to maximize accessibility and efficiency

BraytonHughes Design Studios

away from the windows. Materials and furnishings simultaneously reinforce the desired image of understated elegance. A sampling of the most visible flourishes would include the ice birch used for wood paneling and custom furniture, figured pear wood ornamenting the boardroom table and executive offices, Calacutta Oro stone topping conference tables and files, and fine wool carpet covering the entire floor. Of course, many critical details have been deliberately designed to minimize their presence. Because the building is designed on an atypical, 5-foot, 1-inch module, the additional inch is subtly incorporated in such interior design elements as the wood and glass office fronts, acoustical ceiling tiles and light fixtures. Similarly, the conference rooms' state-of-the-art technology is concealed whenever it is not being employed, so tables hide power/data outlets to avoid detracting from the millwork. A projection screen and projector drop from the ceiling only when needed, and wireless technology provide invisible Internet access and teleconferencing. The result is an uncommonly responsive business environment that enables employees to focus on what matters most throughout the working day.

Above left: Open workstations.
Far left: Private office.
Left: Detail of rotating screen.

CBT

CBT

Analysis Group, Inc.
New York, New York

While many businesses move from private offices to an open floor plan, the new New York office of Analysis Group, designed by CBT, illustrates why many organizations still need them. Analysis Group, which provides economic, financial, and business strategy consulting to law firms, corporations, and government agencies, is a prime example. Founded in 1981, the business currently employs over 430 professionals, most with advanced degrees in economics, law, finance, accounting, and business, who work closely with experts at leading universities. Daily activity in the New York office combines intensive individual effort with collaboration and teamwork. All individual offices are private, yet group around such public spaces as conference and meeting rooms, lounge and pantry, to keep everyone in touch. To ensure an open, accessible and intimate environment, clear glass office fronts maximize daylight and views, zigzagged corridors break up the building's length, and unique materials, patterns and graphics promote a lively feeling. The cool, contemporary interior of glass, teak wood, lightblocks, fabric, carpet, wallcovering and classic modern furniture basks in the soft, warm glow of daylight supplemented by illuminated ceilings, indirect cove lighting and other lighting techniques, ensuring Analysis Group an appropriate home in America's leading financial center.

Above: Informal meeting room.

Left: Large conference room.

Lower left: Private offices.

Lower right: Conference room connection to pantry.

Opposite: Pantry and seating area.

Photography: Anton Grassl/ Esto Photographics.

Analysis Group
Chicago, Illinois

Getting daylight to interior offices and maximizing views was a priority for the Chicago office of Analysis Group, a consulting firm which provides economic, financial, and business strategy consulting to law firms, corporations, and government agencies. With sweeping perspectives of Lake Michigan and the new, widely acclaimed Millennium Park as incentives, the firm retained CBT to completely redesign its new office. The results are visible throughout the private offices, conference rooms, reception area and café of the newly remodeled

facility. Interior offices, for example, now have frameless glass fronts that seem all but invisible inside the 8-foot by 10-foot spaces. In addition, a new café and lounge hugs the perimeter so the office's employees can all see Millennium Park. This means that the office's spatial organization, starting with a public zone at one end that becomes progressively more private at the other, doesn't sacrifice daylight and views for privacy. Better yet, the workplace environment is consistently dynamic, contemporary and attractive, thanks to a design scheme

of bright colors, fine finishes like cerused oak, lacquer and bronze accents, and classic modern furniture.

Above: Café and lounge.
Top right: Conference and reception.
Above right: Entry.
Right: Private offices.
Opposite: Conference room.
Photography: Anton Grassl/ Esto Photographics.

CBT

Accenture
Boston, Massachusetts

As dynamic members of a global management consulting, technology services and outsourcing company, Accenture's consultants spend the majority of their time working off-site or embedded within their clients' offices. The challenge for Accenture in developing a new, Boston office, designed by CBT, has been to attract employees and demonstrate a genuine sense of place. The design succeeds by fostering interaction, communication and reflection on numerous levels. A vigorous sense of connectivity is nurtured through a café, which acts as the central community space for business meetings and social gatherings, glass walls and dividers, and floating staircase. Yet the need for more intimate settings is also generously acknowledged through innovative individual "hotelling" workstations and collaborative "huddle rooms" that are sequenced throughout the environment along with more conventional conference rooms, training room, board room, inviting kitchen and lounge, and signature fish tank. Furnishings also reflect the wide spectrum of choices in the corporate environment by combining contemporary lounge-style furniture with paint, stone, metal, ACT, plaster, carpet and wood floors. To reinforce to visitors the connection between Accenture and the City of Boston, there's even a 10-foot by 4-foot interactive display wall in the elevator lobby.

Top right: Hotelling workstations.

Above right: Huddle room.

Right: Café and lounge.

Below: Individual workstation.

Photography: Anton Grassl/ Esto Photographics.

CBT

ArcLight Capital Partners
Boston, Massachusetts

On one of the top floors of Boston's iconic John Hancock Tower, ArcLight Capital Partners, a fast-growing energy investment firm, experience a unique workplace where transparency and atmosphere prevail figuratively inside and literally outside. That's because the full-floor office designed by CBT, exploits spectacular floor-to-ceiling views of the metropolitan region, changing light and dramatic weather. The project imaginatively blends existing and new construction, creating a lively composition of old and new materials and forms. To unify the enlarged workplace, comprising closed offices, open offices, reception, conference rooms, 30-seat boardroom, kitchen and café, coffee bar and servery, bathrooms, ancillary storage and production space, the design uses new flooring, a transition zone of rich materials, millwork and stone, and a transformed building core. The core, now activated as the hub for reception and other public and social functions, simultaneously connects and subdivides the workplace into distinct zones that share a scheme of perimeter private offices and interior support and production stations. Finished with travertine flooring, carpet, anigre wood, floor-to-ceiling glass interior walls and classic modern furnishings, the space represents an exquisite pinnacle for business.

Above left: Reception.
Above right: Boardroom.
Left: Café and coffee bar.
Far left: Corridor.
Photography: Anton Grassl/ Esto Photographics.

39

CBT

Radius Product Development
Clinton, Massachusetts

For Radius Product Development, an award-winning product design and development firm in Clinton, Massachusetts that collaborates with international clients in the consumer and healthcare industries, the ideal working environment is one many other design firms would surely appreciate. The firm wanted an open studio with a few private offices, conference facilities, model shop, product testing laboratory and gallery/display area. Not surprisingly, that's exactly what it has in its new, three-floor office renovation and expansion, designed by CBT. Yet the facility, occupying a 1950s U.S. Post Office building, is hardly generic. A dynamic stair carves its way through three levels, promoting communications among all design teams. Daylight pours inside from 10-foot high windows and a central skylight. Glass enclosed offices provide acoustical privacy while keeping managers in visual contact with staff. The firm's furniture system came from a rewarding design exercise for staff, is now a great source of ownership. In the end, the wood and concrete floors, glass and steel storefronts, drywall, carpet, contemporary furniture and color palette of black and white with red accents constitute an attractive, versatile and distinctive environment Radius can call its own.

Above: Exterior.
Above right: Interior stair.
Right: Corridor.
Photography: Bruce Martin.

Francis Cauffman

Architecture • Planning • Interior Design

New York • Philadelphia • Baltimore • Syracuse

www.franciscauffman.com

Francis Cauffman

McNeil Consumer Healthcare
Headquarters Renovation/Conversion
Fort Washington, Pennsylvania

The directive from McNeil Consumer Healthcare was simple and compelling. As America's largest producer of over-the-counter pharmaceuticals, including flagship brands such as Tylenol®, Imodium® and Motrin®, they wanted an 'open and dynamic' workspace for their headquarters in Fort Washington, Pennsylvania to encourage better collaboration and cross-functional teamwork. The development of the headquarters workplace transformation initiative started with deliberate preparations encompassing a comprehensive research study of McNeil's business mission, organizational culture and work processes by the design team. Its diligence has been amply rewarded. In a break with precedent, the new and remodeled contemporary facilities have been transformed into a seamless workplace based on function rather than hierarchy. A key design decision was to convert an empty, enclosed exterior courtyard within the core of the building into a highly accessible atrium space which functions as the 'Town Square' of the entire corporate campus. The design provides for both small, informal meetings and the central campus gathering space for large Town Hall meetings and celebratory events such as product launches. This 'Town Square' concept, a product of community based planning, is encircled by 'neighborhoods' consisting of a variety of formal and informal work settings—both open and enclosed—to support collaborative and individual activities. Thus, both onsite and mobile company personnel have a versatile menu of workspaces at their disposal.

Francis Cauffman

A focus of the layout is providing transparency and natural light penetration. This design factor includes the executive area on the second floor which is open to the 'Town Square.' An integral part of the design was the transformation of the visitor's experience. This begins with the new glass and steel entrance canopy, befitting the image of McNeil as a forward-thinking company. The new reception area further enhances the visitor's welcoming experience and highlights the global reach of McNeil through the integration of branding with the architecture. The attractive and comfortable new environment celebrates the employees, customers, the brand and innovative history of the company which is part of Johnson & Johnson, the world's most comprehensive manufacturer of healthcare products. Everything is done with thought. Each detail supports its function-based setting, from the richly nu-anced spatial organization to the versatile materials such as maple wood, aluminum and glass interior partitions with sliding doors, graphic film on glass for privacy and appropriate brand reinforcement, a selection of ergonomic furnishings to the use of a full-spectrum color palette. The result is a work-place which, in the words of McNeil's President, "breathes what McNeil is about."

Top left: Stair in central atrium.
Top right: Touchdown area.
Right: Visitors lobby.
Opposite: Informal meeting hub.

Francis Cauffman

Morris James LLP
Office Relocation
Wilmington, Delaware

Can good design be achieved while maximizing space? The Wilmington, Delaware office of Morris James, a law firm founded in 1931, retained Francis Cauffman to design a new, three-floor, 60,000- square-foot facility for the firms 200+ employees. The new space encourages interaction among the floors and provides amenities for both clients and attorneys whle maximizing real estate. The design supplements such standard law firm accommodations as a reception area, private offices, open workstations, conference center, library and break room. Other features include a hospitality lounge near the reception area that serves as a secondary waiting area for clients, touchdown space, informal meeting place and coffee bar, and communal spaces at circulation paths and connecting stairs where people can pause and talk. Perimeter offices with glass doors transmit daylight to the interior. The award-winning facility, appointed in sapele wood, marble tile, carpet,

glass and drywall, performs so well that an attorney notes, "All my clients have commented on how much they enjoy coming into our new office."

Right: Multi-purpose space.
Below left: Central lobby.
Below: Conference room.
Bottom left: Hallway.
Bottom right: Staff lounge.
Photography: David Lamb.

Francis Cauffman

Morgan, Lewis & Bockius LLP
Support Services Relocation
Philadelphia, Pennsylvania

Co-location is increasingly a state of mind in the global economy. For example, while a prime downtown site remains mandatory for many organizations, it is not always necessary for their support services. Such is the case for Morgan, Lewis & Bockius, a Philadelphia-based law firm with over 1,400 lawyers practicing in 22 offices worldwide. The firm hired Francis Caufmann to design a two-and-a-half-floor, 60,000-square-foot facility to relocate 250 employees of its IT and HR departments. Though both groups had

needs unlike those of the attorneys, the firm sought a facility that expressed their culture within the firm and was determined to share its institutional identity as well as amenities similar to what they previously enjoyed. The modest, yet appealing design, which incorporates private offices, open work areas, conference rooms, community center, data center and elevator lobbies, skillfully implements the firm's design standard, establishes each department's unique identity, and provides flexibility for

future needs. In fact, its multi-functional gathering spaces support an informal and congenial culture that was not expressed previously, and its lighting scheme is more sensitive to the needs of IT staff than before. In the words of an IT employee, "The design of the new space really gives us the flexibility we need."

Top left: Community center.
Top right: Elevator lobby.
Above right: Conference room.
Right: Open workstations.
Photography: David Lamb.

FXFOWLE Architects LLP

FXFOWLE Architects LLP

José E. Serrano Center for Global Conservation, Wildlife Conservation Society
Bronx, New York

What's new at the zoo? Merging with its natural setting at the legendary New York Zoological Park, or Bronx Zoo, while optimizing solar orientation and capturing views, the new, three-story, 30,000-square-foot José E. Serrano Center for Global Conservation, designed by FXFOWLE Architects, provides a timely and appropriate headquarters for 152 employees of the Wildlife Conservation Society. The Society, founded in 1895 and engaged in scientific research, international conservation and science education as well as the management of the world's largest system of urban wildlife parks, needed a new office to unite a diverse mix of programs that had been scattered throughout the Zoo campus. The building program, which included efficient, flexible workspaces, technologically advanced conference rooms, interior and exterior gathering spaces and an information

center, embraced a larger agenda when the Society and FXFOWLE decided to express conservation through the architecture itself. As a result, a sophisticated HVAC system heats and cools the building, daylighting is maximized, and renewable and recycled materials are incorporated so the facility consumes less and lasts longer. The Center's anticipated LEED Gold rating will also demonstrate global conservation in a tangible way that complements the displays at the information center and, of course, the Zoo.

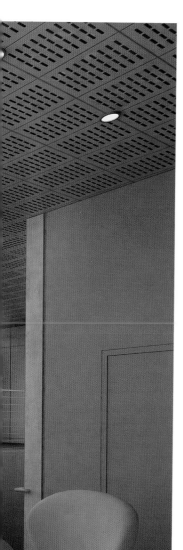

Top: Detail of façade.
Above: Exterior.
Left: Open workstations.
Far left: Entry lobby.
Illustrations: Encore.

FXFOWLE Architects LLP

National Audubon Society
National Home Office
New York, New York

For over a century, the National Audubon Society has been a leading voice encouraging conservation of precious habitat and wildlife for future generations. Audubon has even made an example of its own working environment since the late 1980s by pioneering the practice of environmentally responsible office design. Its newest headquarters, a one-floor, 27,500-square- foot office in New York's up-and-coming Hudson Square district, designed for 100 employees by FXFOWLE Architects, has developed to apply the highest green design standards to achieve LEED Platinum certification for commercial interiors. A sampling of its numerous sustainable features might include the following: low flow and automatic fixtures that reduce water usage; Energy Star appliances for the majority of office needs; under floor air distribution; energy efficient interior lighting and daylight harvesting; wood salvaged or certified by the Forest Stewardship Council as supporting sustainable growing practices; building materials with significant recycled content, such as steel, drywall, carpet and acoustic ceiling tiles; a construction

Below left: Reception.
Below right: Common Area/ Conference Rooms
Opposite above left: Open workstations.
Opposite above right: Private Office.
Photography: David Sundberg/ Esto.

FXFOWLE Architects LLP

waste management plan that has diverted over 75 percent of construction debris away from landfills; quality indoor air enhanced through the use of low-emitting paints, glues, adhesives, sealants, carpet, composite wood and furniture systems; cork and bamboo, specified to encourage the use of rapidly renewable resources; and furniture chosen for sustainability in manufacturing. When Audubon acquired and renovated its last headquarters, 700 Broadway, it produced the first "green building" in New York. Today, 225 Varick Street is a rental property that keeps Audubon on the green leading edge. "We're excited that Audubon is again helping to raise the bar for environmentally-friendly office environments in New York City and beyond," reports Audubon president John Flicker. "We believe that what we've done here, in a leased space, will be a model that can be replicated by more and more businesses and organizations."

Right: Private office.

Below: Individual open work-station.

Photography: David Sundberg/ Esto.

FXFOWLE Architects LLP

SAP America, Inc.
Headquarters Expansion
Newtown Square, Pennsylvania

Business leaders seeking a textbook case study about developing an inspirational workplace that creates much-needed additional space and promotes sustainable design can look to the four-story, 425,000-square-foot expansion of the headquarters for SAP America, Inc., in Newtown Square, Pennsylvania. The two-phase project, designed by FXFOWLE Architects, will deliver new office, meeting, conference and amenity space to over 1,500 employees of the U.S. arm of SAP AG, the world's largest business software company, in a community 15 miles west of Philadelphia. It draws its distinctive features, such as the sensitive placement of its two structures on the wooded site, transparent atrium for dining, meetings and social gatherings, photovoltaic panels, natural ventilation, open offices, ice storage tanks for generating chilled water, green roof and geothermal heating and cooling from SAP America's determination to be a

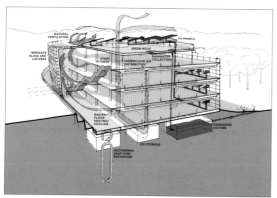

responsible corporate citizen. "With the construction of our new building, we are able to take the lead in making a positive contribution to the environment while providing an innovative, state-of-the-art facility for our workforce," said LuAnn McHugh, vice president, real estate and facilities, SAP America. "We are very proud to be the first corporate-owned LEED Platinum building in the mid-Atlantic region."

Top: Exterior.

Above: Atrium.

Left: Café.

Below left: Sustainable systems.

Ilustrations: Encore (above); Courtesy of FXFOWLE Architects (left).

FXFOWLE Architects LLP

Hosfelt Gallery
New York, New York

Ten years after showcasing work by contemporary artists from all over the world in San Francisco, Todd Hosfelt, owner of the Hosfelt Gallery, in San Francisco's SoMA (South of Market Street Area) district, opened a Hosfelt Gallery in the heart of New York's Hell's Kitchen. Designed by FXFOWLE Architects in association with San Francisco designer Louis Schrump, the facility has been shaped by concepts of spatial flow and abundant daylight. It features a 60-foot-long exhibition space that links two 40-foot by 40-foot galleries. While diffused light from seven skylights accents the space, its individual rooms can still be darkened for such exhibitions as digital installations. The design maintains a dynamic tension between new and old construction, contrasting the new interior walls, which float as crisp, white polished planes free of columns and existing exterior walls, against the dark wood floor and existing rough-hewn wood rafters and cast iron columns. Consequently, the gallery projects a warm yet clean ambience where a variety of contemporary works of art can stake their claim to the New York art scene.

Gensler

Gensler

Nixon Peabody LLP
San Francisco, California

Its old premises were too dark, heavy and circuitous for today's law practice—and it wanted to be America's first law firm with LEED certification. Acting decisively, Nixon Peabody, one of the nation's largest multi-practice law firms, recently developed a new, four-floor, 80,697-square-foot San Francisco office, designed by Gensler, to place 163 employees in a modern, light-filled and open environment and win the coveted LEED certification. The new sensibility is immediately visible in the reception area, where the conference center stands adjacent to the café to open up a "gallery" along the north façade, giving everyone phenomenal views of San Francisco in a space suitable for social events and community outreach. Not surprisingly, innovation is evident throughout the facility. Secretarial workstations, for example, are larger to reflect actual job tasks, printer distribution and file locations are convenient to all members of legal teams, "wayfinding" color walls define circulation paths, and the lighting scheme is enhanced by "light slots" that simulate shafts of daylight. Proud of its LEED certification, Nixon Peabody is duplicating its achievement in projects elsewhere. Declares Tim Blevins, office administrator for Nixon Peabody in San Francisco, "The firm is committed to using sustainable practices on all future building projects."

Above far left: Lunchroom.

Above left: Elevator lobby.

Above: Interconnecting stair.

Left: Reception and conference center.

Below left: Secretarial area.

Below: Breakout area at conference center.

Opposite above: Passage linking elevator lobby and reception.

Photography: Sherman Takata/Gensler.

Gensler

Added Value
Los Angeles, California

The challenge was to unite two once separate business entities, D/R Added Value, a brand development firm, and Kantar Operations, a market research firm, within the former animation studio of Hanna Barbera, the creator of such classic cartoons as The Flintstones and The Jetsons, in Los Angeles. The response: Gensler has designed a unique workspace for 65 employees that straddles the gap between past and present. The budget-conscious renovation of the two-story, 30,000-square-foot California Modernist building, saved by preservationists in 2004, successfully adapts the iconic shapes, colors and textures of the historic structure to meet the goals and culture of Added Value, leaving the infrastructure as untouched as possible.

After the workplace research, visioning sessions and hands-on design development meetings conducted by Added Value and Gensler produced a clear design brief for the facility. Common and inexpensive materials and construction methods were creatively employed to construct the largely open space of asymmetrically placed open workstations, casual meeting areas, private

offices and café/lunchroom. To complete the decidedly playful composition, the interior was finished with a bright color palette and furnishings that represent classics of modernism and retro gestures to the era when Fred Flintstone's shout of "Yabba dabba doo!" reverberated happily across postwar America.

Above, top to bottom: Open workstations, generator room, reception area, café/lunchroom.

Left: Curtain-framed casual meeting area.

Opposite: Casual meeting area with large zebrawood pendant lighting fixture suspended from soffit.

Photography: Patricia Parinejad, Ryan Gobuty.

Gensler

Abu Dhabi Commercial Bank
Abu Dhabi, United Arab Emirates

Abu Dhabi Commercial Bank is a diversified, full-service bank—offering corporate, retail and commercial banking, along with specialized services involving treasury derivatives, infrastructure finance, private banking and wealth management—that aspires to be nothing less than the leading financial institution in the United Arab Emirates. Its ambitious outlook is dramatically displayed in its impressive, new, 25-floor (ADCB occupies 10 typical floors and three executive floors), 230,000-square-foot headquarters designed by Gensler for 600 employees,

in Abu Dhabi. The sleek, European-styled facility, comprising a headquarters retail branch, private offices, client conference suites, staff training facilities, private banking suite and trading floor, is the culmination of a comprehensive effort linking sensitivity to cultural requirements with awareness of world-class and best practices in business. Thus, the needs, aspirations and cultural orientation of customers and employees (40 percent local and 60 percent expatriate) are respected throughout the design. Examples within the orderly,

streamlined environment include integrated prayer facilities, an adaptable desk system that clearly delineates personal space, and lounges within private banking areas that support the region's traditional hospitality. Because the design established workplace standards that did not exist before, it has given the Bank a versatile blueprint for future development as a major financial institution.

Top: Excellency suite waiting area.

Above: Open plan.

Right: Banking hall.

Opposite bottom, left to right: Waiting area, escalator lobby, breakout room.

Photography: Hufton and Crow.

Gensler

EMI Music Japan Ltd.
Tokyo, Japan

How should a physical environment for sound look? The new, one-floor, 30,000-square-foot office of EMI Music Japan, in Tokyo, has been designed by Gensler to house 330 employees of this prestigious Japanese music company (known as Toshiba EMI until it became a wholly owned subsidiary of London-based EMI) in a distinctive spatial hierarchy of sound where music is produced and marketed. The indispensable soundproofed rooms or "sound boxes" for sound listening studios and multi-purpose presentation rooms were placed throughout the entire space as principal design features. The design connects them via the main circulation corridor to form a "sound circuit" that leads from the main reception/café area to the open office and executive area. Everyone—especially artists—is welcomed in the new space, which forges a single identity for the new EMI brand image while respecting the separate identities of the ongoing record labels. Besides having private offices, open office space, meeting rooms, café lounge and communications bar, the space includes artist rooms and other accommodations for promoting artists that can be used for press conferences and parties. As for shaping an appropriate visual environment for music, EMI Music Japan's suave, sophisticated and contemporary design looks and sounds world class.

Right, top to bottom: Artist room in executive area, café, listening room, main reception.

Photography: Nacasa & Partners, Atsushi Nakamichi.

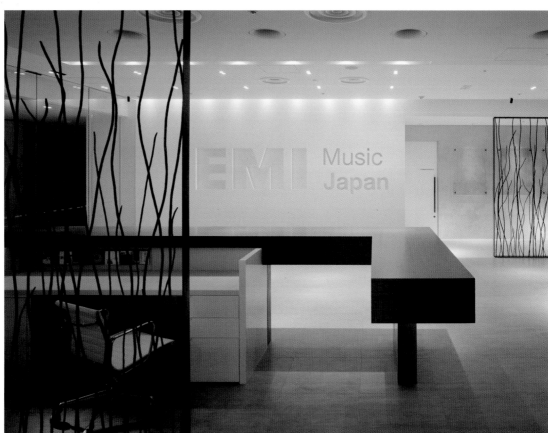

Gerner Kronick + Valcarcel, Architects, PC

443 Park Avenue South • New York, NY 10016 • 212.679.6362 • 212.679.5877 (F)

www.gkvarchitects.com

Gerner Kronick + Valcarcel, Architects, PC

Clarins
New York Headquarters
New York, New York

As a French medical student opening a beauty institute to "take beauty seriously" by offering women personalized treatments and advice, Jacques Courtin-Clarins founded Clarins in 1954 based on combining the best aspects of nature with the benefits of science. Not only did Courtin-Clarins' plant-based skin care products and innovative application methods meet with immediate success, Clarins would become one of Europe's leaders in skin care products, make-up and perfume. Today, the company fields an expanding international network of 20 distribution subsidiaries, a presence in 150 countries, a work force of 6,100 employees, some

Right: Boardroom with logo depicted by glass inset in bamboo.

Below right: Sweeping arc of hall wall with custom displays.

Far right: Reception area with display cabinets leading to conference rooms.

Photography: Eric Laignel.

19,000 points of sale and net sales approaching the $1 billion mark. As a result, such brands as Clarins, Thierry Mugler, Azzaro and Stella Cadente are well known and highly regarded in the United States. Indeed, American shoppers would easily recognize the identity of the new, two-floor, 35,000-square-foot New York headquarters for Clarins USA Inc., designed for some 80 employees by Gerner Kronick + Valcarcel Architects. The facility, comprising a reception area, private offices, open workstations, conference rooms, classrooms, cafeteria, private dining room, pantries and terrace, is as effective as the company's products because of its assured handling of space, materials and lighting. Besides integrating the company's images, icons and products into the workplace environment, showcasing products in ever-evolving displays, the design creates a strong sense of community

Gerner Kronick + Valcarcel, Architects, PC

Above: Stair from main office floor to classrooms and café.

Right: Café with full pantry and coffee bar.

Far right: Open workstation area.

among staff by establishing neighborhoods clustered around cul-de-sacs within the loft-like space, linking these units through a series of corridors or "boulevards" that even draw out occupants of private offices. Its contemporary spirit stresses clean surfaces, minimal detailing, sustainable materials and complexion-sensitive lighting to reflect the Clarins approach to beauty. Occasional pops of the famed Clarins red and intense splashes of the pastel blue and green signature colors of the newly acquired brand, MyBlend, accent calm, natural colors and neutral textures. Individual interiors of bamboo, maple wood, glass, woven carpet of natural fibers, polished concrete slab, terrazzo and a mix of classic Modernist and contemporary furniture continually remind employees and visitors how well nature can be enhanced with the benefits of science—in space and Clarins products.

Gerner Kronick + Valcarcel, Architects, PC

Kushner Companies
New York City Offices
New York, New York

When you own and manage over five million square feet of commercial and residential properties in the northeastern United States, as is the case for the Florham Park, New Jersey-based Kushner Companies, you tend to have very specific objectives for the spaces you develop for your own operations. So

when Kushner Companies retained Gerner Kronick + Valcarcel, Architects, PC to design its new, one-floor, 8,000-square-foot office in midtown Manhattan, it asked for an open environment that would facilitate better internal communication and promote a modern image through a clear, minimal design. The

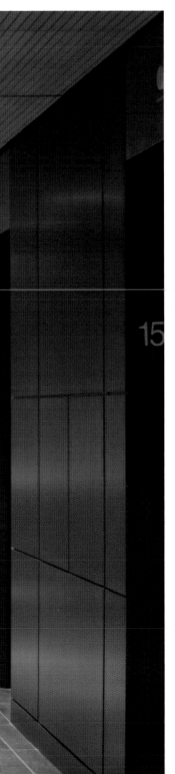

elegant, understated space, consisting of a reception and waiting area, private offices, open workstations, conference rooms, trading desk and pantry, represents a highly precise, aligned and coordinated composition that seamlessly fulfills its objectives within the parameters of an existing office building. Many of the walls, especially those separating perimeter spaces from corridors and interior spaces, use cool sheets of floor-to-ceiling glass to transmit natural light, outdoor views and a sense of openness deep indoors. The overall character of the modular design is enriched by subtle earth tones, timeless materials

Below left: Elevator lobby and reception desk.

Below right: Waiting area.

Bottom right: Executive boardroom.

Photography: Eric Laignel.

Gerner Kronick + Valcarcel, Architects, PC

such as stone, wood and stainless steel, stylish modern furnishings, and architectural lighting that, while largely concealed, cause the walls and floors to glow with warmth and sophistication. For Kushner Companies, a real estate investor with a diverse portfolio of office, industrial, leisure, retail and hotel properties as well as various residential communities, the new facility offers quiet assurance that it knows and exploits the power of space.

Above: Bullpen with trading desks/interior office reception.

Right: Reception area.

H. Hendy Associates

4770 Campus Drive • Newport Beach, CA 92660 • 949.851.3080 • 949.851.0807 (F)

www.hhendy.com

H. Hendy Associates

El Pollo Loco
Corporate Headquarters
Costa Mesa, California

"El Pollo Loco" is Spanish for "The Crazy Chicken" – there's nothing crazy about the growing 400+ unit restaurant chain currently serving California, Arizona, Nevada, Texas, Colorado, Oregon, Washington, Utah, Illinois, Georgia, Virginia, Connecticut and Massachusetts, where customers savor El Pollo Loco's signature citrus-marinated, flame-grilled chicken and fresh Mexican entrees. Indeed, when the company developed its new 100-person, one-level, 25,000-square-foot headquarters in Costa Mesa, California, it wanted a superior workplace. H. Hendy Associates created a contemporary design that drove the company's desire to correct problematic existing conditions such as an overload of file cabinets, high furniture panels, poor ergonomics, insufficient daylight in internal areas, minimal conference facilities – and no lunch room. The colorful new headquarters places uniformly-sized private offices in the interior, open workstations along the perimeter, and file cabinets at designated areas. Huddle, conference, and breakout areas, all named for different Mexican states, are placed throughout the office. And, since the business celebrates food, there's even a festive, centralized kitchen break area adjacent to hotelling workstations defined as "dine in" (reserved) and "drive thru" (unreserved). El Pollo Loco's field people plug in their laptops and work effectively at the "dine in" work stations, and office staff members hold informal meetings in the Lounge and in the open seating areas. Communication has improved, teamwork has improved, and, finally, everyone feels like they have a comfortable and productive work area. The open ceiling, the easy traffic flow, and the visual links to the El Pollo Loco brand give the company the look and feel they wanted. The fresh new environment is a hit with employees. Says El Pollo Loco president/CEO Steve Carley, "This space achieved all of our goals and more."

Top left: Open office area.
Above left: Gallery.
Above right: Entry/lobby.
Opposite below left: Kitchen break area.
Opposite below right: Boardroom.
Photography: Lawrence Anderson.

74

H. Hendy Associates

Kho + Patel
San Dimas, California

When does a certified public accountant's office not resemble one? Ask Kho & Patel, a public accounting firm in San Dimas, California, which serves clients throughout Los Angeles, Orange, San Bernardino, and Riverside counties. The firm recently commissioned H. Hendy Associates to design a 10,000-square-foot, two-floor office that is functionally driven, yet looks "like a design firm." Not surprisingly, the firm had other requests for the contemporary space, including custom workstations, an open coffee bar, a fitness room, and a combined lunchroom/training room. The lunchroom/training room is a large and open multi-use space adjacent to reception where the firm conducts training sessions, holds weekly staff luncheons, and where clients can help themselves to coffee. To promote openness and collaboration, custom workstations are located along the perimeter windows and private offices are on the interior, with glass partitions and void of doors. Jay Patel, owner of Kho & Patel, concludes, "It's amazing what a difference the new place has made in our attitude and the image we project."

Top left: Reception.
Top right: Open workstations.
Above right: Private offices.
Below right: Stair.
Bottom right: Large conference room.
Opposite: Reception and large conference room.
Photography: Lawrence Anderson.

H. Hendy Associates

CO-OP Financial Services
Rancho Cucamonga, California

CO-OP Financial Services, the nation's largest credit union service organization, recently found itself on a very tight schedule. The Ontario, California-based credit union EFT network and processor lacked time to purchase a building or erect a "build to suit" to provide much-needed space. To develop its new, three-floor, 75,000-square-foot facility for 100 employees in Rancho Cucamonga, the organization worked closely with H. Hendy Associates to lease a speculative office building that was ready for construction and upgrade its design, materials and technology. (The long-term investments would precede the conversion of the lease to a purchase agreement.) A formidable challenge was the lobby, a major public space in a facility containing universal "one-size" workstations, conference center, training room and lunchroom. To make it work, square footage was added for a reception area, security was reinforced to accept an ATM with imaging for training visiting credit unions, and accommodations were provided for a receptionist/switchboard operator and security guard. What's particularly impressive is that the project's fresh, contemporary environment, combining such fine materials as wenge wood, marble and limestone with classic modern furnishings and sophisticated lighting, functions as a highly effective workplace with no trace of the velocity that produced it. It won awards from IES for (1) 2008 Energy and Environmental Design Award and (2) 2008 Lumen Award for Excellence in Lighting Design.

H. Hendy Associates

Corporate Business Interiors Inc.
Irvine, California

Left: Entry lobby.
Below: Showroom.
Below middle: Hospitality center.
Bottom: Conference room.
Photography: Lawrence Anderson.

What's good for the customer is good for the staff in the new, one-floor, 6,000-square-foot showroom of Corporate Business Interiors, in Irvine, California, designed by H. Hendy Associates for one of southern California's leading contract office furniture dealers and the Golden State's leading Allsteel dealer. The handsome contemporary space simultaneously dramatizes the dealership's diverse product line and provides an improved and sustainable work environment for its staff. Its design solution confidently models the fluid interior with strong, angular lines, refined architectural details, a range of textural finishes, and a battery of lighting fixtures from a local lighting distributor to draw customers from one vignette to the next. Hugging the glazed perimeter walls, the showroom's largely open floor brings daylight into interior areas and suffuse such facilities as the conference room, hospitality center and special product display areas with a natural glow, flattering people and furnishings alike. Hice Stiles, principal/CEO of Corporate Business Interiors, voices the impressions of his colleagues in saying, "The reactions from our customers, industry partners, architects, and designers who frequent our showroom have been remarkable. Our business has increased along with increased opportunities. We are ecstatic about the results and extremely happy that we chose H. Hendy Associates."

HLW International LLP

New York: 115 Fifth Avenue, 5th Floor • New York, NY 10003 • 212.353.4600 • 212.353.4666 (F)

Los Angeles: 1556 20th Street • Santa Monica, CA 90404 • 310.453.2800 • 310.453.7020 (F)

London: 29/31 Cowper Street • London EC2A 4AT • United Kingdom • 011.44.207.566.6800 • 011.44.207.523.4625 (F)

Shanghai: Section E, 14th Floor • Jiushi Renaissance Mansion • No. 918 HUAI Hai Road (M.) • Shanghai, P.R. China 200020

011.8621.6415.9437 • 011.8621.6415.9438 (F)

www.hlw.com

HLW International LLP

Dechert LLP
Philadelphia, Pennsylvania

Having opened its first office in 1875, Dechert, an international law firm with over 1,000 attorneys, employs office design strategically. Consider its new, eight floor, 220,000-square-foot Philadelphia office, designed by HLW International. After evaluating the facility's programming, Dechert requested a unique environment that would represent a world class international law firm, provide a better experience for everyone, and promote communication. HLW fulfilled these goals in developing 129,000 square feet for the Practice of Law, 16,000 square feet of Law Library, 7,000 square feet of administrative offices, 7,000 square feet of cafeteria and kitchen, and 54,000 square feet for operations/support/records, as well as such ancillary spaces as elevator lobbies, reception and corridors. The facility provides exceptional support for its employees. Office workspace, for example, gives everyone access to daylight without compromising organization, function and privacy. Similarly, the reception area projects a warm welcome through abundant daylight and a magnificent view of Philadelphia's skyline. The internal stair connects all floors to encourage communication and the Practice of Law floors place non-cornered partners in two-windowed offices, eliminating the need for an additional floor. This approach allowed all lawyers, including first and second year associates, to have their own window office, facilitating a "better experience for all."

Top left: Lobby.

Right top to bottom: Stair meeting area; cafeteria; reception; associate's office (Practice of Law meeting area).

Opposite: Entrance.

Photography: Adrian Wilson/Interior Photography.

HLW International LLP

Warren Wixen Real Estate
Brentwood, California

Can a previous tenant's construction be successfully transformed into a new home for an incoming organization? It happens all the time, but Warren Wixen Real Estate, a southern California real estate brokerage, discovered that working with a pragmatic, creative, and comprehensive design firm makes a big difference. HLW International was retained to adapt a small, one-floor, 2,656-square-foot facility in Brentwood for ten employees. The renovation installed five private offices, four open workstations, a reception area and break room without any sign of strain into a shell building which had a dated storefront system, large structural columns and an existing HVAC main loop cutting into the tenant space. The design team incorporated clean, modern and sophisticated furnishings that embrace soothing white tones, custom cantilevered desks that add to a feeling of openness, and a usable pantry/break room that provides panoramic views of the Santa Monica Mountains.

A new lighting scheme of wall washers and general ambient lighting completed the makeover by shedding a flattering light on the revitalized space.

Left: Conference room.

Right top to bottom: Open workstations; executive office; reception area; private office.

Opposite: Lounge as seen from reception.

Photography: © Michael Schmidt Photography.

HLW International LLP

Schroders
Project Invigor
London, U.K.

Schroders, a global asset management company offering clients "200 years of forward thinking," is not the only organization whose premises have increased to function effectively or project a timely image. However, the venerable institution (founded in 1804) has wasted no time undertaking a comprehensive modernization of its 950-person, nine-floor, 180,000-square-foot London office, designed by HLW International. The new scheme decisively solves such problems as lengthy internal travel for hosts and guests from ground floor entrance to top floor meeting rooms, the lack of a place for staff to congregate, and the empty atrium in the building's center. In restacking Schroders, HLW has turned the entire ground floor into a new meeting suite adding conference rooms and a much-needed multimedia auditorium to reception and concierge facilities, recast the atrium as a new staff café and general meeting space, opened up floors of private offices and open workstations with new breakout and meeting areas, and inserted a new internal staircase to encourage staff interaction. Every detail was considered, including the new and refurbished furniture complementing such new finishes as limestone, red gum veneer, plaster, back-painted glass, ceramic tile and carpet. That may be why visitors generously praise the renovation—along with employees.

Above left: Reception.
Above right: Seating area.
Below left: Artwork gallery – Nasdaq.
Below right: "Mood" conference room with red lighting.
Opposite: Atrium.
Photography: David Churchill.

HLW International LLP

Citigroup
Shanghai Headquarters
Shanghai, China

An environment of understated elegance arrayed against an optimistic backdrop of limitless space gives the new, eight-floor, 128,000-square-foot Shanghai Headquarters of Citigroup, designed by HLW International, an appropriate setting where 1,200 employees pursue long-term prospects. Championing simplicity and transparency, the design features such highly visible spaces as the 35th floor reception lobby. Here, a long expanse of clear glazing lets visitors enjoy spectacular, unobstructed skyline views of the booming metropolis. (Opposite this wall, a deep gallery zone delineates the lobby's boundary by providing an overflow space with informal meeting areas inside a richly patterned, linear wood enclosure.) Elsewhere, virtually all architectural partition walls parallel to the

exterior wall are glazed, and private offices and meeting rooms are generally located against the central core wall or set back from the exterior wall to minimize visual obstructions. There is more to the interior than glass, of course. To generate a lively contrast in materials, the emphatically modern design plays soft fabrics on seating, light-colored carpet and warm finish colors against sleek glazing, high-tech metal ceilings, contemporary casegoods and stainless steel hardware. Glazed interior walls also incorporate sealed integral motorized blinds to quietly impose their presence whenever this transparent setting needs privacy.

Top left: Elevator lobby.
Top right: Reception.
Above: Conference room.
Left: Break area.
Photography: Shen Zhonghai.

HOK

HOK

How can a workplace be designed to accommodate a well-established company with a decidedly youthful, creative spirit? For MediaCom, a Toronto-based advertising agency, the new, three-floor, 46,000-square-foot office, designed for 250 employees by HOK, provides a spirited and satisfying answer. The design transforms a typical office tower interior into the kind of industrial-style, loft-like environment associated with high-technology startups to enhance team interaction. Standard and innovative office components, including reception, private offices, the Work Space, an open, community-based workplace, team rooms, boardroom and the Bistro, a two-story, high-energy space for food service, meetings, town halls and client presentations, combine to give Media-Com numerous options for activities. To impart a unique image, HOK has employed such design techniques as a deconstructed ceiling with exposed building elements, wood ceiling joists, dropped ceiling planes, and suspended light fixtures over workstation areas, along with classic Modern furniture and such materials as Douglas fir plywood, narrow-profile, T-bar ceiling system, suspended fluorescent light fixtures, garage doors and Magic Glass®, which transforms the boardroom's walls from transparent to opaque with the flip of a switch. MediaCom's people are understandably proud of their new office, a response other creative organizations can readily appreciate.

MediaCom
Toronto, Canada

Right: Bistro seating.
Below right: Team room.
Bottom left: Elevator lobby.
Bottom right: Reception.
Opposite: Bistro and connecting stair.
Photography: Richard Johnson.

HOK

SJ Berwin
London, UK

A leading pan-European law firm, employing over 170 partners and 500 lawyers throughout the continent, SJ Berwin is justifiably sensitive to the working environment. The London office's recent move to a former HSBC building, where 800 employees occupy a new, award-winning, five-floor, 220,000-square-foot space designed by HOK, demonstrates its concerns. Reception areas, enclosed offices, client meeting and entertainment facilities, staff restaurant, "grab and go" café, sleep pods with showers, and 25,000-square-foot roof terrace with 90-seat marquee capability, all satisfy very specific requirements. Floors follow modular configurations, for example, to provide flexibility across the large floor plates, with desirable views of St. Paul's Cathedral and the Thames River shared universally as breakout spaces. In addition, seminars held in the seminar suite can use adjacent meeting rooms for refreshments, aiding post-seminar networking and selling. Classic contemporary furnishings provide the finishing touches to the design. While the bench desking system serves multiple office configurations, accompanied by custom designed meeting tables, matching bookcases and iconic modern seating, the sophisticated lighting makes even core areas seem naturally illuminated. Consequently, the interiors, appointed in European oak, solid surfacing, clear and obscured glass, and painted steel, project a perfectly stunning image for this major leading-edge firm.

Right: Café.
Below right: Small conference room.
Bottom left: Elevator lobby.
Bottom right: Large conference room.
Opposite: Helical stair.
Photography: Peter Cook, Nick Gutteridge.

HOK

AOL
Beverly Hills, California

More than a workplace, the new, two-and-one-half-floor, 65,000-square-foot AOL regional headquarters for 155 employees in Beverly Hills, designed by HOK, helps attract and retain top talent and communicates a new brand image and corporate identity for the Internet service provider and media company. The award-winning space blends pizzazz with pragmatism. Its private offices, open workstations, teaming areas, Internet café, hotelling stations, huddle rooms, brainstorming areas and broadcast studio constitute three zones: studio production areas, work areas

and branded areas. Not only does this arrangement convey AOL's market presence and technological sophistication, it overcomes such building constraints as the lobby rotunda, which bisects all floors, and low ceiling heights. Studio production areas occupy the ground floor flanking the lobby rotunda, where their black and white setting offers a neutral backdrop for complex technology. By contrast, work areas are warm and corporate, featuring cherry wood accents, and branded areas such as the ground floor Internet café, touchdown area and studio prefunction area, and second

floor coffee bar and huddle rooms promote louder and more collaborative interaction. If the contemporary furnishings, accented by classic modern pieces, epitomize "fresh," "current" and "hip," you heard it here first.

Above left: Touchdown stations.

Above right: The second floor rotunda, a casual meeting area.

Upper right: Work area with director office.

Right: Open workstations work area, under vault on third floor.

Opposite: Internet café.

Photography: Benny Chan/ Fotoworks, Scott MacDonald/ Hedrich Blessing.

HOK

Nina Footwear
Corporate Headquarters
New York, New York

It's true: Women's fashion footwear is still being designed and manufactured in 21st-century America. Sophisticated women in the United Kingdom, Canada, Australia, Asia, South America and the United States can be seen wearing products by Nina Footwear, a New York-based, family-run company founded in 1953 that currently operates factories in Spain and China. In fact, Nina Footwear recently moved into a new, two-floor, 30,000-square-foot corporate headquarters,

designed by HOK that could help extend its global reach. The contemporary facility comprises executive offices, design studios, showrooms, reference library and lunch area for 110 employees in a spacious, collaborative and branded environment quite unlike the company's previous workplace. Besides offering the staff a supportive environment, Nina Footwear now gives visiting buyers privacy through individual showrooms, provides new branding for each brand as a cohesive design element,

and connects designers to the company's legacy in an archival room that accommodates 9,000 pairs of shoes. Efficiently organized with the design/showroom on the third floor and the executive, marketing and operational functions on the fourth floor, the space has genuinely inspired its occupants. Declares Scott Silverstein, CEO of Nina Footwear, "HOK's design has drastically improved the way we conduct business."

Top left: Branding wall.
Top right: Brandin wall/show-room entry.
Upper left: Showroom.
Left: Stair and reception.
Photography: Peter Paige.

Huntsman Architectural Group

50 California Street, Seventh Floor • San Francisco, CA 94111-4677 • 415.394.1212 • 415.394.1222 (F)

48 Wall Street, Fourth Floor • New York, NY 10005 • 212.693.2700 • 212.693.2123 (F)

www.huntsmanag.com

Huntsman Architectural Group

Kimball Office
San Francisco, California

A new, one-floor, 5,000-square-foot showroom in San Francisco's Financial District does more than extend the presence of Kimball Office, a major national office furniture manufacturer respected for its wood furniture. The contemporary facility, designed by Huntsman Architectural Group, also enables Kimball Office to showcase its metal furniture systems before design firms and businesses in this key neighborhood. Its stylish and reconfigurable space deliberately courts both audiences. Since architects and interior designers specify furniture for clients' offices, the showroom presents products in dynamic settings that emphasize their quality, adaptability and sustainability. Yet the space caters to business people as well by presenting the furniture as an essential component of the actual office environment used daily by the staff. Everything seems visible and accessible wherever visitors stand. Once they notice the bold window display, featuring the Kimball name in large-scale letters against a 14-foot-high oak wall, they are drawn inside by such devices as the branding gallery, highlighting the showroom's sustainability initiatives, and a bright, poppy-colored feature wall at the back. Commenting on how effectively the showroom functions, Jeff Fenwick, vice president/general manager of Kimball Office, declares, "Huntsman gave us everything we asked for and more."

Top: Wood workstation with conference room behind.

Above: Featured metal workstation display.

Right: Center of showroom.

Opposite: Entry corridor with oak feature wall.

Photography: David Wakely.

Huntsman Architectural Group

Dfm
San Francisco, California

For over 80 years, San Francisco Bay Area offices have favored custom-crafted wood casegoods and seating made by Dfm, a regional brand competing in a market dominated by national manufacturers. To ensure future success, the San Leandro, California-based company retained Huntsman Architectural Group to design a new showroom in San Francisco's Embarcadero district. The six-person, ground floor, 1,300-square-foot facility is near many design professionals so they can see products in person, and is conveniently located for dealer representatives visiting clients throughout the region. Its design scheme highlights the fabrication process, much as the San Leandro factory showroom does, to remind designers and clients that products can be customized to satisfy functional needs or aesthetic visions. This philosophy produces a cruciform floor plan comprising of product displays on one side and a studio for representatives, designers and clients on the other. Equipped with a work table that doubles as a cabinet for finish samples, the studio zone provides a public area in the front and staff area in the back. Because architectural elements are treated like fine furniture using wood, stone and other quality materials, Dfm's showroom and products form a superbly crafted, total environment that visitors enjoy exploring. To quote Kevin Sarkisian, Owner and President, "Our standard products have never stood so proud."

Above Right: Entire showroom.

Right: Workroom with furniture display wall.

Below: Casegood display.

Opposite: Exterior signage display.

Photography: David Wakely

Huntsman Architectural Group

Mercedes-Benz of San Francisco
San Francisco, California

So sleek, functional and appropriate is the new, two-story, 72,000-square-foot automobile showroom and maintenance center for Mercedes-Benz of San Francisco, designed by Huntsman Architectural Group, that customers may not realize it combines buildings that once housed KQED Public Television and Public Radio with new construction. The transformation, a consolidation of all business and customer-related functions and services in one facility, dramatically enhances the dealership's effectiveness and profile. The transformation began when the architect analyzed on-site buildings to determine their potential function on the urban auto dealership's campus. After the study identified buildings worth retaining, their structures were modified to combine them into a comprehensive new scheme. The studio's offices and later an auto parts store, for example, stood on the corner of a busy intersection, making it the logical showroom. With its second floor removed and original fenestration widened and fitted with low-iron glass (for maximum transparency and accurate color rendition), the storefront now houses a three-story cylindrical glass tower which displays new models and serves as a beacon to the nearby highway. Yet its interior, like its exterior, is seamlessly integrated into a continuously open, light-filled, and easy-to-navigate environment. What is

Right: Guest lounge.

Below: North-facing exterior façade.

Opposite: Atrium between showroom and sales offices.

Photography: David Wakely.

Huntsman Architectural Group

especially impressive about the minimal contemporary design, which encompasses showroom, reception, guest lounge, service and maintenance, and administrative offices, is its rich variety. From the loft-like showroom (enclosed by glass beneath a soaring ceiling), towering glass atrium (separating showroom from sales department), and guest lounge (covered by glass panel staircase and baffled by fountains), to the sales offices (modeled as floating cubes), the design blurs the lines between showroom and workplace. Interior appointments intentionally give pride of place to the luxury cars on display while complementing their industrial aesthetic with clean lines, neutral colors, and a sympathetic vocabulary of glass, aluminum, ceramic tile, stucco and boardform concrete. David Barsotti, Owner of Mercedes-Benz of San Francisco, lauds the award-winning facility by observing, "Having such a great space to work tends to bring us the best and brightest employees."

Above: Feature wall in atrium.
Right: Reception desk.
Photography: David Wakely.

Ken R. Harry Associates, Inc.

Ken R. Harry Associates, Inc.

Skadden Arps Slate Meagher & Flom LLP
Houston, Texas

Left: Elevator lobby.
Above: Breakroom.
Below left: Main conference room.
Bottom left: Reception.
Opposite: Reception seating.
Photography: Joe Aker, Aker/ Zvonkovic Photography.

Having successfully opened its Houston office in 1991, Skadden Arps Slate Meagher & Flom LLP, a prominent, New York-based law firm with over 2,000 attorneys and 22 offices on four continents, recently asked Ken R. Harry Associates to help expand its presence in Texas by designing a new, one-floor, 25,091-square-foot office for 63 Houston employees. The stylish, modern design deftly resolves numerous challenges. Its spatial organization, for example, separates public spaces from private work areas by placing attorneys in private perimeter offices,

support staff at open workstations within the interior, and guests in the conference center, enjoying access to reception, conference rooms and food service. In addition, wood, leather and stone combine with patterned glass to extend a "Texas welcome" to guests: portals resembling "outstretched arms" or inverted "L"s enliven the elevator lobby and reception seating area, new furniture and wood finishes harmonize with existing furniture, and custom tables created by the design team give the main conference room unprecedented flexibility to recon-

figure. How well does the new facility perform? John C. Ale, managing partner of the firm, notes, "Our clients and visiting colleagues always walk away impressed—and the latter with a tinge of envy!"

Ken R. Harry Associates, Inc.

Schlumberger Information Solutions
SIS Breakthrough Performance Center
Houston, Texas

The oil industry has trusted Schlumberger, the world's leading oilfield services provider, for help in exploration and production since 1926, inspiring Schlumberger Information Solutions to unveil a unique way for clients and partners to experience cutting-edge E&P software and services technology. Its new, one-story, 8,000-square-foot SIS Breakthrough Performance Center, in Houston, has been designed by Ken R. Harry Associates to invite customers to collaborate in developing groundbreaking technologies. But where design could easily have created attention-getting conference rooms

with support facilities, video conferencing rooms, "Navigation Dome" and reception area, the facility deliberately mutes physical space to let Schlumberger's technology shine. The Innovation Laboratory and executive briefing center that constitute the facility's key components are crafted as precisely as high-tech instruments, to be sure, employing such quality materials as stone, stainless steel, wood veneer and patterned glass to create a sleek, contemporary environment. Nowhere is this concept more apparent than in the Navigation Dome, where an 16-foot wide by 9 -foot high 3-D high-definition screen

presents Schlumberger's premier software in a cool, crisp setting. Praising the blend of high performance and aesthetic restraint, Dan Ronan, PE, business development manager of SIS, says, "The Breakthrough Performance Center showcases Schlumberger's technological leadership."

Top right: Reception.
Above left: Navigation Dome.
Above right: Computer room.
Bottom left: Partner wall.
Opposite: Elevator lobby.
Photography: Nick Merrick/ Hedrich Blessing.

Ken R. Harry Associates, Inc.

Liskow & Lewis
Houston, Texas

Can offices anticipate growth? It's a serious question for law firms, as the Houston office of Liskow & Lewis knows. A regional law firm founded in 1935 that has over 100 attorneys and offices in Lafayette, Louisiana, New Orleans and Houston, Liskow & Lewis retained Ken R. Harry Associates to design its new, one-floor, 27,541-square-foot office in downtown Houston's First City Tower. The office's population expanded from seven attorneys to over 20 during the design and construction phases. To avoid the financial burden real estate often places on growing law firms, Liskow & Lewis adopted a flexible, "one size fits all" office standard for partners and associates alike. Another innovation for this contemporary environment, which features a reception area, private offices, open administrative spaces, conference center, lunch room and support services; small, but efficient touch down offices in the conference center where clients and/or visiting attorneys can conduct business. Thus, both public and staff areas provide attractive and functional surroundings with generous daylight and views, stylish materials and furnishings, clear material boundaries for visitors, and excellent artificial lighting.

To quote Robert Theriot, a shareholder of Liskow & Lewis, "Our utilization and enjoyment of the space has been more than we imagined."

Top: Exterior of large multi-purpose room.

Above left: Mingling area in conference center.

Above right: Large Multi-purpose room.

Opposite: Entry from elevator lobby.

Photography: Nick Merrick/ Hedrich Blessing.

Ken R. Harry Associates, Inc.

Winstead PC
Houston, Texas

Picture an office projecting an image of excellence, integrity and commitment to clients, where attorneys and clients can conduct business in a comfortable and inviting atmosphere. This ideal is a daily reality for 278 employees in the Houston office of Winstead, one of the largest business law firms in Texas, with 300 attorneys and offices in the state and Washington, D.C. However, the five-floor, 96,674-square-foot facility, designed by Ken R. Harry Associates with private offices, conference center, mock courtroom, support services, reception and lunchroom, faced numerous on-site challenges. For example, because the elevator lobby is deep inside the core, a series of barrel-vaulted portals shortens the long path to reception. Daylight penetrates the interior through patterned glass walls enclosing the conference rooms. Stationing pairs of legal secretaries before a high-density file room gives lawyers immediate access to some 20 files each. To serve multiple functions and save space, the mock courtroom's judge's bench and jury railing can be stored behind a movable wall. Observing the new facility's effectiveness, Cindy Graves, CLM, Winstead's director of administration, declares, "Our offices give our visitors a powerful image of who we are as a firm and provide a clear message about our brand."

Above left: View from elevator lobby towards reception desk.

Top right: Mock courtroom.

Above: Reception area.

Photography: Nick Merrick/ Hedrich Blessing.

LS3P ASSOCIATES LTD.

LS3P ASSOCIATES LTD.

Copper Station Holdings
Ridgeland, South Carolina

Working outdoors sounds like a fantasy that would be quite impractical for most organizations. Yet there's an unmistakable outdoor feeling inside the new, 8,500-square-foot office for Copper Station Holdings, a land real estate brokerage in Ridgeland, South Carolina, designed by LS3P ASSOCIATES LTD. That's because the owners deliberately linked their passion for nature with their appreciation of contemporary design. Involving the owners and staff, the design team developed an airy scheme that organizes the space—compromising private and open offices, reception/lobby, gallery, small conference room, lounge, kitchen/break room, fitness room, restroom/showers, print/copy and storage—around the boardroom making sure each employee has "a room with a view." The result is attractive and practical. Not only does it compensate for its remote location, providing the convenient fitness room and well-stocked kitchen/break room, but it also celebrates nature through forest-inspired colors, renewable materials such as wood panels and trim, palm wood flooring, hand-made paper artist luminaires and cleanly detailed furnishings. The conference table is hewn from a single tree trunk, still displaying its natural, undulating edges, infusing a modern interior with an al fresco spirit.

Top left: Restroom/shower.
Top right: Boardroom.
Above right: Open office area.
Right: Kitchen/break room.
Opposite: Reception lobby.
Photography: Matt Silk.

LS3P ASSOCIATES LTD.

Greystar Real Estate Partners
Charleston, South Carolina

Would a company that combines four traditional lines of real estate—investment, development, construction and property management—into one young, energetic and fast-growing business, develop a headquarters that is similarly traditional and contemporary? That's what you'll find at the new 6,500-square-foot office for Greystar Real Estate Partners, in Charleston, South Carolina, designed by LS3P ASSOCIATES LTD. The 32-person facility, consisting of reception, enclosed and open offices, conference rooms, restrooms/showers, kitchen/copy and utility spaces, graces its 1911 landmark building with Neoclassical architecture accented by "contemporary interventions." In effect, the design puts a modern spin on its conventional configuration of private perimeter offices and open-plan interiors. For example, private offices, enclosed in sleek, steel-and-glass partitions stretching from the heart-pine floor to the exposed ceiling and HVAC system, give everyone views of historic Charleston's rooftops. Open-plan workstations, crafted of cypress wood in classic profiles, stay low to emulate the "trading floor" energy of the young staff. Historic furniture blends with modern pieces to reinforce the positive tension between old and new. Exposed MEP systems complement the building's concrete structure above open-office areas but disappear behind a suspended ceiling of stretch vinyl in public areas. Has the past ever looked this timely?

Top left: Conference room.
Top right: Restroom/shower.
Above left: Executive offices.
Above right: Open-plan workstations.
Opposite: Corridor.
Photography: Matt Silk.

LS3P ASSOCIATES LTD.

Decision One Mortgage-HSBC
Fort Mill, South Carolina

Far left: Private office.

Left: Executive boardroom.

Below: Main lobby.

Opposite top right: "Bus stop."

Opposite middle right: Break-out workspace.

Opposite bottom right: Entrance lobby.

Photography: Tim Buchman.

Designed to support mortgage lending through independent brokers, the new five-floor 182,000-square-foot office of Decision One Mortgage-HSBC, located in Fort Mill, South Carolina, was designed by LS3P ASSOCIATES LTD. What the award-winning contemporary facility doesn't reveal, however, is that its development proceeded as swiftly as the business activity that followed. Because timing was critical, the project's six-month design phase overlapped the 10-month construction schedule. The project became more demanding just as the core and shell were emerging from the ground and the interior architecture was leaving the conceptual stage, when the owner decided to attain LEED® certification. Consequently, the 900-employee facility comprising public areas, private offices, meeting and conference rooms, training classrooms, cafeteria, data processing, copy/scanner rooms and fitness center, provides sustainability—LEED Silver—as well as flexibility, multi-functioning and comfort. Spatial organization is appropriately uncomplicated, with support functions occupying a long, rectilinear building core with open office spaces surrounding them, punctuated by "bus stops," or printer areas, and private offices filling strategic corners. Mike Tarulli, director of HSBC Corporate Real Estate, N.A., praised LS3P saying, "Thanks for your attention to detail on the economics of this project—no small feat considering the schedule, LEED and many other moving pieces."

LS3P ASSOCIATES LTD.

National Gypsum
Headquarters Renovations
Charlotte, North Carolina

In a sweeping renovation designed by LS3P ASSOCIATES LTD., National Gypsum, one of the world's leading gypsum wallboard producers, has transformed the 12,000-square-foot ground floor of its 350-person headquarters, in Charlotte, North Carolina, into an impressive, contemporary showcase of its products. The completion of the project, involving new lobby entrances, exhibit space, formal and informal meeting spaces, sales conference room, employee café and outdoor dining area, has integrated displays of both employee and corporate culture into the building's primary entry. To overcome existing spatial constraints, the design incorporates every available building element into the overall scheme—including the columns and the once hidden ceiling structure, now exposed with floating soffits to raise the ceiling height—and unifies the multiple environments through the introduction of a defining gypsum board ring linking all public spaces together. Not only does the project equip the integrated building products manufacturer with state-of-the-art facilities for various gatherings, it displays the versatility of National Gypsum wallboard and other products for walls and ceilings. Amidst interiors appointed in stylish, modern furnishings with a color palette based on the corporate colors, red, yellow and gray, National Gypsum convincingly demonstrates why it has been an industry leader since 1925.

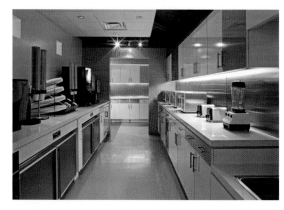

From top to bottom: Main entry and logo wall, exhibit corridor, conference room, café servery area.

Photography: Tim Buchman.

Margulies Perruzzi Architects

308 Congress Street • Boston, MA 02210 • 617.482.3232 • 617.482.0374 (F)

www.mp-architects.com

Margulies Perruzzi Architects

HLM Venture Partners
Boston, Massachusetts

Aesthetics matter in the global economy, and the one-story, 10,000-square-foot Boston office for 22 employees of HLM Venture Partners, designed by Margulies Perruzzi Architects, offers striking proof. Boston and San Francisco-based HLM, a venture capital firm that specializes in early- to mid-stage healthcare business start-ups, hired Margulies Perruzzi Architects to change its brand image from Neo-colonial to modern within its existing space. In addition to updating the aesthetics, the renovation resolves the isolation previously felt among people at the ends of the floor by introducing large expanses of glass, curved surfaces at transition points and a colorful, curved soffit encircling the core. The design also differentiates public and private areas, while creating an accessible gathering place by relocating the reception area to a central space directly off the elevator lobby. Interestingly, the new environment is as rich and warm as before, owing to such details as cherry wood millwork, spectacular views of Boston's Back Bay seen through the abundant glass, contemporary furniture and original art that replaces Neo-colonial furniture and museum art reproductions, distinctive lighting fixtures, floors of plush carpet and marble tile, and the soffit's red arc sweeping through the office, displaying the color of the company's logo like a proud banner.

Top to bottom: Reception desk, hallway flanked by private offices, casual meeting space, and reception area.

Opposite: Border between public area and office spaces.

Photography: Warren Patterson.

Margulies Perruzzi Architects

Nuvera Fuel Cells
World Headquarters
Billerica, Massachusetts

Above: Open workstations.

Left: Conference room, corridor and common area.

Below left: Casual sitting area.

Bottom left: Breakout space.

Opposite: Tour path.

Photography: Warren Patterson.

Thomas Edison, the Wright brothers and Steve Jobs would probably feel at home in the new, one-floor, 110,684-square-foot world headquarters of Nuvera Fuel Cells, in Billerica, Massachusetts, designed by Margulies Perruzzi Architects. The project transforms a former warehouse into the combined office, laboratory and factory of a global leader in fuel cell technology. Housing closed and open offices, 25 state-of-the-art R&D laboratories, more than 50,000 square feet of manufacturing space, train-ing center, café, shipping/receiving area, mechanical room, lobby and common spaces, the new headquarters roughly doubles Nuvera's space for a Billerica staff projected to grow from 100 to more than 350 in the next five years. Fulfilling this agenda involved transitioning engineers from private offices to an open plan environment that is adjacent to flexible, interchangeable laboratories and manufacturing activities they can monitor through large windows. To bring all employees together and encourage interaction, a broad central hallway that facilitates plant tours reaches all areas of the building, complemented by "big boxes" containing conference rooms and other needed support services, and a centrally-located café and mailroom. Declares Jeff Cook, Nuvera's manager of facilities and laboratory operations, "Margulies Perruzzi Architects did an excellent job designing our facility around our unique requirements."

Margulies Perruzzi Architects

A Major Insurance Company
Hingham, Massachusetts

Good business and good citizenship happily coexist in a new, four-story, 329,000-square-foot regional headquarters in Hingham, Massachusetts designed by Margulies Perruzzi Architects for 1,000 employees of a major insurance company. The modern glass, stone, precast concrete and metal structure provides cost-effective, comfortable and state-of-the-art space for open workstations, private offices, conference facilities, training center, disaster recovery facility, childcare center, community room and enclosed connector to a 1,184-car parking structure, all organized around a central lobby and multi-purpose space. Yet it transcends conventional standards of excellence by helping employees achieve a better work-life balance, welcoming local residents with dedicated accommodations, and implementing sustainable design. Employees have

noticed the difference immediately thanks to such features as outdoor views, ample daylight, lounges/pantries near workspaces, on-site day care, lockers and showers for fitness enthusiasts and bicycle commuters, ergonomic furnishings and a popular cafeteria in the multi-purpose room. In addition, the design reduces environmental impact through minimal site grading and tree clearance, re-use of native materials for construction, and environmentally sound measures such as energy and cost-efficient building systems, healthy material selections, and low-VOC emitting furnishings. The project has achieved LEED Silver certification, and the award-winning design draws compliments from occupants and neighbors every working day.

Below left: Multi-purpose space.

Below right: Central lobby.

Bottom left: Exterior.

Bottom right: Staff lounge.

Photography: Warren Patterson.

Margulies Perruzzi Architects

A Major Financial Services Company
Boston, Massachusetts

Left: Entrance lobby.

Below: Hallway and open workstations.

Bottom: Reception area.

Photography: Warren Patterson.

Though few office workers might voluntarily relinquish their private offices for open workstations, the new, eight-floor, 243,000-square-foot office for 800 employees of a major financial services company in Boston, designed by Margulies Perruzzi Architects, demonstrates that this major cultural change can be staged smoothly and satisfactorily. The adoption of the new configuration—grouping private offices along the perimeter of the rectangular floor plate and freeing up the corners of the floors—lets daylight and outdoor views spill over the low workstations and throughout the space while providing greater flexibility in future renovations. One reason why the transition proceeded so well was a decision by the company's facility management staff and design team to involve all user groups in identifying needs. Another contributing factor was the quality environment created for the private offices, open workstations, conference facilities, trading floor, reception and pantries. Among its distinguishing characteristics are the use of the company's extensive art collection as a wayfinding tool, such timeless materials as carpet, fabric, porcelain tile, maple wood, granite and glass, contemporary furnishings offering comfort, utility and style, and a sophisticated lighting scheme for task, display and decorative lighting. In fact, the staff consistently identifies this office as the best in the company's portfolio.

McCarthy Nordburg

McCarthy Nordburg

Delta Dental of Arizona
Corporate Headquarters and Service Center
Glendale, Arizona

Delta Dental of Arizona, a nonprofit organization founded by the Arizona State Dental Association in 1972, keeps the Grand Canyon State smiling by covering over 435,000 people through some 1,800 employer groups. A new, two-story, 31,350-square-foot build-to-suit office building in Glendale features interiors designed by McCarthy Nordburg to keep Delta Dental's corporate headquarters and service center running smoothly. Working closely with Delta Dental and other members of the building team, McCarthy Nordburg has created a cohesive workplace for employees that is effective and inviting. From the dramatic, two-story lobby, where classic lines and bold material contrasts are softened by diffused glass and warm wood tones, to the private offices, open workstations and conference rooms, which share the lobby's design vocabulary at a more intimate scale, the contemporary design balances a warm welcome with the need for security, privacy and efficiency. Thus, internal support core elements are used to discreetly separate the executive wing from the service center. How successfully the building team has served Delta Dental of Arizona, a member of the nationwide Delta Dental Plans Association, can be gauged by the stringent budget—$6 million for total construction—and brisk timetable—23 months from design through construction.

Top: Reception desk.
Above: Conference room.
Left: Lobby stair.
Opposite: Reception/lobby.
Photography: A.F. Payne Photographic/McN.

130

McCarthy Nordburg

Visitor Information Center
Phoenix, Arizona

What would you like to know about fast-growing Arizona and its vibrant capital, Phoenix? Developing a new, highly visual and multi-media approach to informing the public about their resources, destinations and activities was one of two major challenges in developing the new Visitor Information Center in Phoenix. The other was coordinating the goals of the Center's two sponsors, the Greater Phoenix Convention & Visitors Bureau, a private, nonprofit group, and the Arizona Office of Tourism, a state government agency. None of these issues are apparent in the finished space, of course. Visitors to the new, one-floor, 2,500-square-foot facility, designed by McCarthy Nordburg, delight in the contemporary, simple-flowing space, where architecture, human interaction and new technology blend seamlessly. The street-level space offers visitors different ways to inform themselves: desktop computers for Internet access, a staffed information desk with printed literature, and a multi-screen video wall comprising nine 50-inch plasma screens. While curving walls and soffits give it a distinctive shape, it can quickly adapt to new uses. Virtually all key interior elements, for example, are designed to be easily relocated or removed. All the public has to do is to step up and enjoy the show.

Below: Multi-screen video wall.
Opposite top: Desktop computers.
Below right: Information desk.
Photography: McN/Immedia.

McCarthy Nordburg

Hacienda Builders
Scottsdale, Arizona

Beautifully designed, well-built, master crafted homes have been the hallmark of Hacienda Builders since Todd Stevens and David Cohen founded it in 1991 to serve Arizona's Valley of the Sun. In its new, two-story, 35,000-square-foot, company-owned headquarters in Scottsdale, designed by McCarthy Nordburg, Hacienda Builders has room to house its progressive and growing organization and to showcase its construction. Families come to the facility to select the construction materials, building systems, and other options and services for homes the company will build for them.

Consequently, the design employs soffits and floor finish transitions to enable the office space and the design center, where families see vignettes of residential interiors, to flow together in form and function. Not only does the use of natural stone, wood and other fine materials with natural and artificial lighting in the relatively open space enhance its volume and create a welcoming feeling, it affirms the quality of the company's homes. Families see these intimate design elements everywhere, from the building lobby to the office and design center. Interestingly, the design

center incorporates custom furniture that replicates residential pieces to illustrate residential applications while providing commercial office functionality, resulting in a unique home away from home.

Left: Lobby.

Below: Design center.

Opposite: Reception and office.

Photography: Michael Norton Photography.

McCarthy Nordburg

Healthcare Administrative Company
Headquarters and Service Center
Phoenix, Arizona

There's a new "front door" to the corporate offices and main service center of a major healthcare administration company, located in Phoenix, that serves the entire Southwest region. It's part of an extensive renovation and expansion, designed by McCarthy Nordburg, that adds 4,000 square feet of new construction to a 250,000-square-foot campus that consists of four interconnected buildings and one satellite building. Besides giving the campus a formal entry it has greatly needed, the new architectural rotunda lobby connects two existing buildings and creates synergy within the organization by merging two distinct operational groups. The design functions on both functional and symbolic levels. The state-of-the-art conference room that is a key component supports multi-media presentations, teleconferences and video screenings with a superbly crafted architectural composition of woodwork and wallcovering panels that houses and conceals all the electronics. Appointed in warm wood tones, subtle color palette, and direct and indirect lighting, the overall space creates an inviting atmosphere for long meetings that is dignified without being overpowering. At the same time, the rotunda element invokes a memorial-like feeling that communicates to employees and visitors the importance of their work and whom they are ultimately supporting.

Mojo•Stumer Associates, P.C.

Mojo•Stumer Associates, P.C.

Cline Davis Mann, Inc.
New York, New York

Left: Track lighting trough.

Far left: Concealed control panel.

Below: Viewing screen.

Opposite below: Glass wall panels.

Opposite bottom: Soffit reveals.

Opposite bottom right: Ceiling detail.

Overleaf: Video presentation mode.

Photography: Mark Stumer/ Mojo•Stumer Associates.

Even without knowing about Cline Davis Mann, consumers of healthcare products reaffirm its unique position daily as a leading creator of world-class healthcare brands. The New York-based company was founded 22 years ago as a medical advertising agency, and has developed a specialized organization to guide healthcare brands from the prelaunch market seeding to the end of product life cycles. Its command of the field—handling more billion-dollar brands than any other agency serving the healthcare industry—is expressed in two new conference rooms, designed by Mojo•Stumer Associates. Each room, seating 16 or more, is a complex assemblage of IT, A/V, communications and lighting technologies for multi-media presentations. However, what invariably impresses clients is the interior architecture surrounding the high-tech equipment. Fully intended as "knockout" environments, these superbly crafted examples of contemporary cabinetmaking and millwork use the ceiling plane—articulated as convex curving soffits—and walls as sculptural motifs. Of course, along with such sleek finishes as wood, leather, stainless steel, aluminum, stone and carpet, there are custom details like the painted glass panels that double as writing surfaces and pin-up boards with clips for pads, demonstrating that form can shape function as well as follow it.

Mojo•Stumer Associates, P.C.

Community National Bank
Woodbury, New York

While nobody expects today's banking halls to resemble the Neo-Classical temples of yesteryear, banking customers understandably still favor traditional signs of security and trust wherever they deposit their money. The desire to balance lively modern design concepts with timeless banking themes has produced an exceptionally attractive space at Community National Bank's new, one-floor, 3,8 00-square-foot retail store in Woodbury, New York, designed by Mojo•Stumer Associates. Housing the third branch of an institution

founded in 2005 as a full service commercial bank, offering a wide array of deposit and loan products, the Woodbury space is a compact design comprising a tellers' counter, open work areas, conference room and manager's office. The facility feels larger than it is because the design skillfully manipulates its boundaries through multiple wall and ceiling planes. No expanse of wall runs long before being interrupted by another located closer or further from the center of the space, for example, while wall surfaces keep changing from wood to

glass or drywall—the latter painted white or the bank's signature blue. Overhead, soffits and coffers tease the eye by altering the ceiling's height. Shouldn't a bank promising highly personalized service have a branch offering many points of view?

Below left: Seating area.
Below right: Overall view.
Opposite above left: Entrance.
Opposite top right: Tellers' counter.
Photography: Mark Stumer/ Mojo•Stumer Associates.

Mojo•Stumer Associates, P.C.

Barley Ziecheck Medical Offices
New York, New York

Hospitals are increasingly taking cues from hotel and residential design to make their environments more patient-centered, user-friendly and inviting, so it's not surprising that doctors' offices are following suit. At the new, one-floor, 3,500-square-foot Barley Ziecheck Medical Offices, in New York, Mojo•Stumer Associates has designed a functional and cost-effective space that extends an immediate welcome to patients. The facility, which includes a reception area, waiting room, examination rooms, consultation rooms, manager's office and business office, makes the most of its tight budget through crisp, minimal detailing, basic building materials, selective use of wood and marble trim, hospitality-style furnishings, and the doctors' modern art collection to introduce a feeling of quality and comfort. Its spatial orientation is straightforward, based on centering the circulation around the spacious waiting room and locating doctors' offices along window walls, simplifying wayfinding for patients and staff alike. Keeping the waiting room airy and open has also yielded an important bonus for the practice. Because the elevator opens directly into the waiting area, the sight of what could easily be perceived as a residential living room comes across as warm and sociable—a sight that patients everywhere wouldn't mind seeing.

Above right: Corner detail.
Right: Art gallery
Below left: Waiting room.
Below right: Wall detail.
Photography: Mark Stumer/ Mojo•Stumer Associates.

NELSON

MediaVest
New York, New York

What kind of workplace suits an energetic, youthful and creative organization? Can the facility also improve efficiency, increase density and upgrade finishes—despite a tight construction budget and schedule? For MediaVest, a leading media specialist in brand building, the newly remodeled, four-floor, 100,000-square-foot space in its New York office, designed by NELSON, answers these questions with utility and style. The renovation places a reception area, private offices, open workstations, conference rooms, coffee bar and other public spaces in a bright, lively and contemporary environment. Such details as warm colors, metallic finishes, wood veneers, frameless glass office fronts, frosted glass for meeting spaces,

epoxy floors, contemporary furniture and indirect lighting closely support both individual and team-focused activities. In the reception area, for example, the striking, sculptural look created by the furnishings is accented with sleek, flat monitors to welcome visitors and encourage impromptu gatherings. Similarly, a sweeping wall of wood and painted white sections defines and separates the executive conference room, incorporating custom millwork and integrated AV systems, from the adjacent coffee bar, highlighted by a white seating island and blue floor. Individually or together, the facilities give MediaVest the kind of options any organization needs in a fast-moving world.

Above: Coffee bar.
Left: Executive conference room.
Far left: Partitioning wall.
Photography: Chun Y. Lai.

NELSON

Comerica Headquarters
Dallas, Texas

Everything is "bigger in Texas." But when Comerica, the financial services firm founded in Detroit in 1849, relocated its corporate headquarters to Dallas, the company asked NELSON to design a five-floor, 210,000-square-foot facility with a refined, traditional interior that demonstrated an "elegant restraint." Both qualities are evident in the beautifully detailed space, which includes the Atrium and openly adjacent first floor banking center as well as floors two through five in

Comerica Tower, previously known as Bank One Center. Such varied spaces as the reception lobbies, boardroom, private dining, and multiple conference, training and office environments display abundant evidence of skilled cabinetmaking—featuring choice woods accented by marble and granite—that are perfectly complemented by traditional furnishings and historic regional art and antiques. Yet the facility benefits no less from specialty services Comerica requested from NELSON. Not only has

NELSON helped install the necessary high-tech security system, it has introduced state-of-the-art lighting and lighting controls that have resulted in unprecedented visual effects. Thanks to the new lighting, the large, semi-circular glass ceiling atop the fifth-floor atrium has changed from a dark, dreary structure to a vibrant and sophisticated barrel vault, celebrating the timeless spirit that now infuses Comerica Tower.

Above left: Boardroom.

Right, top to bottom: Executive conference room, executive reception, executive prefunction.

Opposite: Atrium at fifth floor.

Photography: Mark Scheyer, Inc.

NELSON   Financial Office and Call Center
San Antonio, Texas

Left: Executive waiting area.
Below: Central lounge.
Opposite: Reception.
Photography: Mark Scheyer, Inc.

Sustainable design means many different things to a growing roster of "green" building projects and their building teams. In a financial office and call center in San Antonio, designed by NELSON, "green" elements are evident throughout the 55,000-square-foot interior of an old warehouse that has been given new life itself as a certified LEED Silver renovation. The relocation of these financial functions dramatically improves working conditions for the multiple teams now deployed in the new facility's 270 general open office workstations, 84 call center workstations, support areas and executive offices. Whereas the six floors of the branch's former premises segregated people, discouraged interaction, and offered limited exterior views and access to daylight, the conversion of the single floor of the previously vacant structure, integrating expanses of new windows and clerestories, has enabled the financial institution to improve function, introduce amenities, and create an environmentally responsible and architecturally branded workplace. Better yet, the transformation of the

building reaffirms the client's ongoing commitment to maintain jobs in the region, tighten speed to market and attract top talent. Interestingly, the design's success hinges on the subdivision of the cavernous space, capped by a 26-foot-high ceiling, rather than its sheer volume. The vast scale is broken down into user-friendly neighborhoods, defined by the interplay of high and low ceiling structures and intersecting wall planes, that are linked together by a central spine that clients enter at one end of the long axis and employees at the other. Having such a basic spatial organization is particularly useful given the multiple functions this facility houses, which include strategically placed conference, training and team rooms, main and satellite copy/work rooms, recycling centers, mail rooms and centralized lounge, in addition to the open workstations, call center and executive office area. The client's determination to develop a classic architecturally based interior design that would honor sustainable design principles added layers of complexity to the project. However, the client's unwavering adherence to high standards also proved critical to completing the development, which took just 12 months from project initiation to occupancy.

Above: Call center.
Right: Conference room.

OWP/P

OWP/P

ORIX Real Estate Capital
Chicago, Illinois

After 15 years in the same space, the Chicago office of ORIX Real Estate Capital, an equity and debt capital source for all types of properties nationwide, recently used a move to reposition itself within the real estate community. Its goal: Recruit clients and talent more effectively by fostering collaboration. The new contemporary environment, a one-floor, 22,000-square-foot space designed by OWP/P, clearly transcends aesthetic improvements. Teamwork between staff and clients is actively encouraged, for example, through formal and informal meeting areas clustered off the elevator lobby. The staff, occupying private offices and open workstations, has options for group activity as well, thanks to such facilities as a "live/work" center, comprising a café , library and informal meeting areas, located on main corridors with access to views and food. As real estate is ORIX's business, the thoughtful use of space is demonstrated down to the smallest detail, including such material choices as millwork that contrasts richly grained rosewood against subtle wenge, clear and frosted glass, and fine fabrics and carpeting. A creative way to maximize space can even be found in the boardroom, where benches flip down from the wall only as needed to provide seating for larger meetings.

Top left: Library.

Above left: Break room.

Right: Live/work center.

Above far right: Reception.

Opposite bottom left: Reception screen.

Opposite bottom right: Boardroom.

Photography: Christopher Barrett/Hedrich Blessing.

OWP/P

Convia, Inc./A Herman Miller Company
Office/Showroom
Buffalo Grove, Illinois

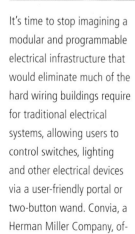

It's time to stop imagining a modular and programmable electrical infrastructure that would eliminate much of the hard wiring buildings require for traditional electrical systems, allowing users to control switches, lighting and other electrical devices via a user-friendly portal or two-button wand. Convia, a Herman Miller Company, of-fers this product now—and proves it in a working office/ showroom. The two-floor, 7,000-square-foot facility in Buffalo Grove, Illinois, de-signed by OWP/P, highlights Convia's versatility among functioning workstations for 15 people, conference areas, informal lounges, bar/kitchen area, mezzanine gallery and equipment test laboratory. The mezzanine, installed so customers can view the sys-tem above the ceiling plane at eye level, is the project's defining element. Besides establishing proximity to the product, it separates guest- and employee-only areas with an arresting, singular form that recalls the iconic molded plywood chairs of Charles and Ray Eames. Of course, it doesn't hurt that the attractive facility's office system and other modern furnishings come from parent company Herman Miller, a legendary and innova-tive furniture maker whose long history with the design community adds credibility to its offspring's entirely new product. To quote Convia's president, Randy Storch, "This is Mecca if you want to see what Convia is about."

Top left: Bar and lounge.
Above left: Lobby.
Above: Mezzanine.
Opposite: Stair and lobby.
Photography: Christopher Barrett/Hedrich Blessing.

OWP/P

Toshiba America Medical Systems
Vernon Hills, Illinois

Software programmers are conventionally walled into cubicles to avoid distracting coworkers. So who is confining the programmers who create software for sophisticated medical imaging equipment at Toshiba America Medical Systems' new, one-floor, 31,000-square-foot office in Vernon Hills, Illinois? No one. In fact, the extensive facility, designed by OWP/P, reflects Toshiba's decision to exchange the traditional model for a space that encourages staff interaction. Its building program, including private offices, open workstations, conference rooms, café and "pods" for casual meetings, has been devised to serve general offices, multiple software development laboratories, and two fully functioning CT scan machines and an X-ray machine, which directly test applications developed at the facility. To inspire and support staff interaction, the space is divided into Tech Zones, housing individual workstations, laboratories and equipment study, and Garden Zones, hosting office breaks

and collaboration, as visibly represented by semi-enclosed pods, where casual seating, marker boards and pin-up areas await informal meetings or breakout sessions. Fresh inspiration has also come from two contextual sources: Toshiba's business,

Top: Pod interior and coffee bar.

Left: Pod exterior.

Above: Garden Zone.

Opposite: Conference room.

Photography: Christopher Barrett/Hedrich Blessing.

OWP/P

producing the software that runs X-ray, ultrasound and MRI machines that "see" into other things, and the company's Japanese ownership, alluded to through subtle reference to Zen gardens. For example, materials of varying degrees of transparency mimic Toshiba's machines by enabling the eye to "see" from one space into another. Thus, pod partition walls and other selected walls throughout the office use semi-transparent acrylic sheets to let light penetrate while exposing their inner structural elements. Chairs of clear plastic with visible metal skeletons create the illusion that their occupants are floating on air, and light fixtures incorporate semi-transparent and translucent lenses that let viewers look inside and through them. Zen gardens are evoked in such low-key ways as the facility's color palette of grays, greens and blues, representing stone, sand, plants and water, and the shape and arrangement of the pods, inspired by the circles raked into the sand. Fitted with sleek, contemporary furnishings and illuminated by daylight from skylights as well as high-tech lighting fixtures, Toshiba's office has gracefully transported its programmers to a brave new world imbued with a calming yet dynamic energy.

Above: Corridor and open workstations.

Partridge Architects Inc.

Partridge Architects Inc.

Logan Circle Partners, L.P.
Philadelphia, Pennsylvania

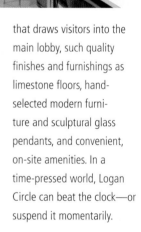

The tension is inescapable on a trading floor, a critical link in today's global financial market where assets are bought and sold to exploit minute-by-minute changes in value. For this reason, financial businesses such as Logan Circle Partners, a Philadelphia-based asset management firm, give

traders specialized workplaces like its superb new, one-floor, 19,500-square-foot office for 90 employees, designed by Partridge Architects. This striking, contemporary environment consists of a trading floor flanked by glass-fronted private offices, reception area, conference rooms, open work areas,

training room and copy/mail room. The minimally detailed yet luxuriously appointed interiors offer employees such amenities as a café, lounge and gymnasium with showers and changing rooms. Logan Circle is clearly a functional space, given the trading floor's advanced technology and

complex infrastructure. Yet it's also a visual statement about confidence, comfort and security— and winner of Best of Show-Financial Services from the Philadelphia IIDA and Shaw Contract's "Design Is" People's Choice Award. Consider its curved wood accent wall with concealed LED lighting

that draws visitors into the main lobby, such quality finishes and furnishings as limestone floors, hand-selected modern furniture and sculptural glass pendants, and convenient, on-site amenities. In a time-pressed world, Logan Circle can beat the clock—or suspend it momentarily.

Top right: Trading floor.
Above left: Lobby and main conference room.
Above right: Café and lounge.
Left: Accent wall.
Far left: Elevator lobby.
Opposite: Reception.
Photography: Jeffrey Totaro.

Partridge Architects Inc.

Center City Film & Video
Philadelphia, Pennsylvania

If viewers of Sprout, a PBS Kids television show for pre-schoolers, were to visit the new, 10,700-square-foot home of the show's producer, Center City Film & Video, in downtown Philadelphia, they would be pleased to find a space that is considerably livelier than the standard corporate interior. The ultra-modern design by Partridge Architects, houses 45 employees of the full-service film, video and interactive production company. Film and video editing suites, voiceover recording booths, audio and sound editing suites, and a studio dedicated to Sprout share the floor with such conventional office facilities as private offices, open work areas, conference rooms, lunchroom, copy/mailroom and server room. Co-locating production and administration requires special detailing, of course. With reception and conference rooms at the front end and studios and production spaces in the building core, private offices are left to surround the perimeter. The production facilities incorporate carefully routed mechanicals and added soundproofing to control sound transmission, as well as exposed ceilings with structural grids to accommodate theatrical lighting. A bold color palette of black, white, red and yellow combines with organically shaped modern furnishings, chosen to contrast with the interior's rectilinear architecture, to complete a dynamic space that adults can appreciate as much as pre-schoolers.

Right: Private offices.
Below right: Sprout studio.
Bottom left: Lobby and main conference room.
Bottom right: Lunchroom.
Opposite: Reception.
Photography: Jeffrey Totaro.

Partridge Architects Inc.

Partridge Architects Inc.
Philadelphia, Pennsylvania

Right: Private office.
Far right: Entrance to lobby.
Below left Lobby.
Below right: Main studio.
Opposite: The "Hub."
Photography: Jeffrey Totaro.

Focusing its expertise, skill and energy on its own behalf, Partridge Architects has developed an exceptional new, one-floor, 7,800-square-foot office in center city Philadelphia. The respected full-service architecture, planning and design firm, founded by architect John Partridge in 1987, successfully achieves two formidable project goals: producing a versatile, unconventional and exciting workspace for 26 employees from a standard office building floorplate, and diligently applying sustainable design practices to win LEED-CI Gold certification. In transforming existing site conditions, the design polished the concrete floor and selectively exposed steel beams, deck and fireproofing to break up the studio and illustrate architectural elements to clients. Another interesting design element is the "Hub," an open pantry and multi-purpose gathering area which serves as Partridge's design, education and social center. Sustainable practices included using recycled construction materials, diverting construction waste from landfills, using zero formaldehyde and low-VOC products, and specifying furnishings that are recyclable and/or have recycled content. The lighting design maximizes daylight, and a master timer and occupancy sensors control energy-efficient lighting fixtures. "Typical" as the office's spatial organization may be, from front-end reception area and conferencing space to back-of-house studio, library and other support facilities, nobody would describe the resulting environment that way.

Partridge Architects Inc.

CB Richard Ellis
Philadelphia Headquarters
Philadelphia, Pennsylvania

Seeking a simple, modern space that would immediately draw visitors inside, CB Richard Ellis recently retained Partridge Architects to design a one-floor, 27,000-square-foot Philadelphia headquarters that is notably airy, open and inviting. The facility houses 80 employees of the global real estate services firm in a basic open plan environment served by multiple conference rooms. Seizing the opportunities offered by the scheme, the design team has treated the conference rooms as focal points and opened a vista from the elevator lobby to the reception area through a floating glass signage wall that reveals sweeping views of the office interior and center city Philadelphia. Clean, crisp architectural elements promote the facility's cool, modern image throughout the open workstations, perimeter private offices, and interior support and storage space. Yet the firm's modern outlook does not preclude a touch of visual drama beyond the conference rooms and signage wall. While a maple wood-paneled accent wall at the reception area brings understated elegance to the reception desk, breakout room, corridor and main conference room, undulating blue soffits envelope the conference rooms and the café/lunchroom in a captivating glow. Don't vision and creativity play legitimate roles in business as well as design?

Perkins+Will

Perkins+Will

Goodwin Procter LLP
Los Angeles, California

Goodwin Procter has transformed itself, from a single office founded in Boston in 1912 by Harvard classmates Robert Goodwin and Joseph Procter, into a national practice of 850 attorneys with offices in Boston, New York, Washington, D.C., and Northern and Southern California. A major thrust of its expansion has been the opening of its second Los Angeles office. This new office in downtown Los Angeles is a one-floor, 20,428-square-foot facility designed by Perkins+Will for 45 employees. The space reflects the attorneys' preference for an environment free of the stereotypes and formal barriers of a traditional law office. Amid private offices, open administrative areas, conference rooms, war rooms, a high-density filing room, and a kitchen/dining space, glass is used to make walls transparent. Neutral colors and timeless materials such as wood and limestone help foster contemplation and comfort, and shoji screens, river rocks and the waterfall behind the front desk of stacked wood planks honor the region's Asian cultural influences. Even the lighting reinforces the unique character of the facility, including cloud-like fixtures in the main conference room and water droplet-like fixtures in the lunchroom. Clearly, Goodwin Procter feels at home in Los Angeles.

Below left: Elevator lobby.
Below right: Reception and main conference room.
Bottom left: Corridor to reception.
Bottom right: High-density filing room wall.

Opposite above left: Reception desk.
Opposite above right: Waiting area.
Photography: Benny Chan/fotoworks.

Perkins+Will

Haworth
Calgary Showroom & Learning Centre
Calgary, Alberta, Canada

A leading producer of systems furniture, seating, storage, wood casegoods, raised access floors and moveable walls for today's workplaces, Haworth is gaining stature in the business world by championing adaptable and sustainable office environments. The company's philosophy is dramatically illustrated in the new, two-story, 22,000-square-foot Calgary Showroom & Learning Centre that adjoins its factory in Calgary,

Alberta, Canada, designed by Perkins+Will|*Eva Maddox Branded Environments* and Busby Perkins+Will. To serve Calgary's booming economy, Haworth needed space for product demonstrations, conferences and offices featuring a range of workplace concepts, product applications and integrated communications systems. Here, Haworth's clients would acquire new ideas through memorable

educational experiences for building more flexible, adaptable and sustainable interiors. A sleek, contemporary "building within a building" anchors the design, with the showroom wrapping around the Learning Centre's sustainability exhibit. The showroom features a full office environment, ranging from enclosed executive offices to open plan areas. The sustainability exhibit comprises four spaces: an informal

gathering space, a showcase for modular construction, a comparison of modular and conventional construction, and a high-tech meeting space. Illustrating Haworth's beliefs with care, expertise and imagination, the facility embraces numerous sustainable design strategies to achieve a USGBC LEED™ Gold certification.

Top left: Sustainable construction lab.

Above left: Refresh area and wood salon.

Above right: Reception and stair hall.

Opposite lower left and right: Client events room entrance to refresh area and wood salon.

Photography: Nick Merrick/ Hedrich Blessing.

Perkins+Will

**Perkins+Will
New York Office**
New York, New York

Tomorrow's office is visible today at the new, one-floor, 12,000-square-foot facility housing 95 employees of Perkins+Will in downtown-Manhattan. This facility, designed by and for the New York office of one of America's most respected design firms—honored with 70 years of award-winning work and the American Institute of Architects Firm of the Year award—actively tests innovative workplace concepts that the firm promotes. For example, every staff member, from principal to intern, has a standard 6-foot by 7-foot workstation in an easily reconfigured workstation bay of fixed spine and mobile furniture. The open arrangement eliminates private offices to promote collaboration, share daylight and views, and provide visual connection. In addition, team rooms along the main corridor support private conversations, phone calls, small meetings and visitor touchdowns, while larger conference rooms

accommodate activities requiring more floor area. Other features are less obvious yet equally important. Not only has the office reduced water usage by 45 percent through water-conserving fixtures, it has minimized energy costs through lighting controls, reused over 30 percent of existing

furniture, and improved air quality with low-VOC emitting materials. Such efforts have earned Perkins+Will a LEED-CI Gold rating, numerous design awards—and employees' gratitude.

Right: View of flexible conference room from reception.
Below left: Reception.
Below right: Open studio.
Bottom left and right: Conference room, team room.
Photography: Eduard Hueber/ archphoto.com

Perkins+Will

TELUS Corporation
TELUS House Atrium
Vancouver, BC, Canada

One of Canada's leading telecommunications company with 10.3 million customer wireline and wireless connections, TELUS Corporation also acts as a major corporate supporter of Canada's charitable and non-profit organizations. Appropriately, TELUS' recent renovation of the nine-story, 130,410-square-foot William Farrell Building, in downtown Vancouver, for office and retail use simultaneously revitalizes a key neighborhood and creates a potent corporate symbol. The latest project at TELUS House, designed by Busby Perkins+Will Architects, introduces a revamped, 248-foot-high, 4,536-square-foot atrium for employee use, a dramatic architectural transformation incorporating seismic upgrading and green design. The double-glazed, fritted structural silicone capless glazing system supported by a tensile steel structure maximizes available daylight while minimizing heat exchange. In addition, a new, elegant steel structure increases the building's structural integrity, while two pedestrian bridges and a folded-plate steel stairway encourage employees to circulate. As for interior furnishings, a raised floor system adds flexibility and simplifies reconfigurations; custom designed lighting fixtures provide quality, energy-conserving illumination; low-VOC carpet, paint and adhesives improve air quality. Coffee kiosk, café and lounge furniture, custom designed by Busby Perkins+ Will Architects, offer utility, style and value—qualities TELUS customers surely endorse.

Right: Atrium with double-glazed wall.

Below, left to right Pedestrian bridge, lounge seating and planters, coffee bar.

Photography: Martin Tessler.

Lauren Rottet - Architecture and Design

180 Varick, Suite 404 • New York, NY 10014 • 212.537.9245

555 South Flower Street, Suite 700 • Los Angeles, CA 90071 • 213.612.4585

808 Travis Street, Suite 100 • Houston, TX 77002 • 713.221.1830

3338 M Street NW, Second Floor • Washington, DC 20007 • 202.621.7830

50 California Street, Suite 1500 • San Francisco, CA 94111 • 415.277.5487

20645 North Pima Road, Suite 200 • Scottsdale, AZ 85255 • 602.293.6089

1.866.629.4284

www.rottetstudio.com

Lauren Rottet - Architecture and Design

Paul, Hastings, Janofsky and Walker
London, U.K.; New York, New York;
Paris, France; Shanghai, China

Above: Conference center, New York.

Left: Seating area, Shanghai.

Far left: Reception, London.

Below: Reception, New York.

Opposite: Stairs, New York.

Photography: Eric Baingel (London, Paris), Michael Moran/ Michael Moran Photography (New York), Grzegorz Kosmal/ Rottet Studio (Shanghai).

Corporate America's overseas drive has profoundly affected the nation's law firms. Consider the evolution of Paul, Hastings, Janofsky and Walker. Founded in Los Angeles in 1951, Paul Hastings is one of only two major U.S. law firms formed after World War II among the top 25 in America. Ranked 18th in the United States and 23rd in the world in *American Lawyer*'s 2007 survey, it has over 1,200 lawyers and 18 offices in America, Europe and Asia. Lauren Rottet has facilitated the firm's growth by designing eight of its offices. As illustrated by new facilities in London, New York, Paris and Shanghai, Rottet Studio's award-winning work has centered on the unified design scheme that reflects Paul Hastings's corporate identity, branding efforts and

organizational culture. This approach tactfully incorporates local design cues so clients can readily identify with each facility. In London, the firm's 68-person gateway to its European practice, a one-floor, 7,000-square-foot renovation exploits the visibility of the London sky

through a glass roof and atrium to transform the reception area and conference rooms. Enclosures chiefly of clear glass with opaque surfaces stand back from corner intersections, perimeter walls and internal atrium to obscure indoor and outdoor boundaries, in contrast to

seating and conference tables in natural materials, deep colors and textures. Similarly, the new, 11-floor, 110,000-square-foot New York office acknowledges its building's off-center core, irregular, angled corners and non-uniform column spacing. Interior support spaces,

private perimeter offices, double-height atrium, forced perspective corridors, and interconnecting staircase make the workplace feel more spacious than it actually is to the 475 employees of Paul Hasting's largest office. For the finishing touches, contemporary furnishings custom

Lauren Rottet - Architecture and Design

designed by Lauren Rottet, FAIA complement wood, stone, metal and other timeless materials. The 134-person Paris office, by contrast, occupies an historic limestone building in the fabled 8th arrondissement where walls cannot be reconfigured. The design thus focuses on furniture, cabinetry and creative lighting, using careful planning to separate public reception rooms from private practice areas. Following

European custom, the floor plan accords the law library a prominent place, and the eclectic interiors blend classic furnishings and restored original lighting fixtures with sleek custom conference tables and seating and new lighting to achieve a dynamic equilibrium. Finally, the 175-person, two-floor, 56.307-square-foot Shanghai office salutes its base building with such quality finishes as wood, stone, carved lacquer

and accent rugs, giving private perimeter offices and interior support spaces the requisite look of respectability and success.

Projects of Lauren Rottet while with DMJM Rottet.

Upper right: Private office, Paris.

Right: Conference room, Paris.

Lower right: Reception, Paris.

Below: Staircase, Paris.

Opposite: Seating area, Paris.

Lauren Rottet - Architecture and Design

Global Management Consulting Firm
Houston, Texas

Left: Elevator lobby facing main conference room.

Below left: Large open area.

Below: Office corridor.

Opposite upper left: Reception.

Opposite upper right: Break room.

Photography: Joe Aker/Aker/Zvonkovic Photography.

Can a workplace promote an organization's core values of teamwork and collaboration? A global management consulting firm recently asked Lauren Rottet to design such an environment for 165 employees in Houston. The result is a lively, two-floor, 32,000-square-foot facility in a downtown high-rise that encourages group activity. To energize an environment that includes private offices, conference and training rooms and an employee lounge, the flexible, modular scheme offers a range of common areas for informal and formal gathering, including team rooms at the corners of floors and between office suites, and large open areas just off the elevator lobby, including the reception area and the main gathering area facing the main conference room.

Their notable effectiveness reflects sensitive detailing and adaptability. A figured wood veneer, for example, is used as a motif to link together the adjacent reception area, main gathering area, central staircase and employee lounge. Movable partitions let the main gathering area quickly convert from entertaining or cafeteria configuration to training. Of course, the entire facility supports teamwork, from the glass fronts of private offices, which establish an open, vibrant quality, to the ergonomic contemporary furniture, which combines comfort and style, optimizing working conditions wherever employees convene.

Project of Lauren Rottet while with DMJM Rottet.

183

Lauren Rottet - Architecture and Design

Investment Management Firm
Los Angeles, California

Designing the five-floor, 100,000-square-foot renovation of the 500-person Los Angeles office for an investment management firm may not sound particularly challenging in general terms. But consider the specific conditions imposed on Lauren Rottet during a recent assignment to remodel a space for private offices, trading rooms, conference and teleconference facilities, training rooms, kitchen and café areas, and common reception area. First, the firm's goals for the facility were to create an environment of the highest design quality—one completely free of ostentation—that would be simultaneously flexible, visually open and user-friendly. In addition, the project would restack the existing floors while maintaining uninterrupted daily operations within the facility during construction. Finally, no individual or group of employees could be moved more than twice, areas surrounding construction had to look as if no construction were occurring, and end users could not be impacted by construction activity. That Lauren Rottet met the firm's requirements with distinction, starting the four-phase construction project in fall 2006 and completing it in fall 2008, is evident in its ongoing relationship with the client. Lauren Rottet has been asked to design more offices for the firm in Los Angeles, Orange County, California, San Antonio and Phoenix.

Project of Lauren Rottet while with DMJM Rottet.

Above left: Breakroom.
Above right: Open office space.
Below left: Main reception.
Below right: Reception area.
Photography: Jimmy Cohrssen.

RTKL Associates Inc.

RTKL Associates Inc.

Gibraltar Bank
New York, New York

Clients know their business is valued at Gibraltar Bank, a Coral Gables, Florida-based private bank founded in 1994 that is an affiliate partner of Boston Private Financial Holdings. Gibraltar develops branch banks such as its new, 3,800-square-foot installation in New York, designed by RTKL Associates, to resemble high-end residences. Accordingly, the compact Manhattan facility, which provides bank tellers, private offices, open work areas, conference rooms, bank vault, employee lounge and restrooms for 13 employees and visiting clients, reserves nearly half its square footage and all views of prestigious

Park Avenue for public/client areas to create an appropriate ambiance. Because the entire branch is high end with no "back of house," individual spaces are highly efficient and fastidiously detailed. Thus, some private offices are quite small, security and openness are carefully managed through sight lines and custom designed metal screens, teller lines are low and accessible, and conference rooms are as comfortable as living rooms. In addition, wood parquet insets in marble flooring, Art Deco-inspired chandeliers and luxurious, residential-style furnishings embellish elements of the

Gibraltar brand, including the reception area colonnade, signature red color, and artwork relating to the branch's location, celebrating Gibraltar's presence in the nation's financial and cultural center.

Below left: Conference/living room overlooking Park Avenue.

Below right: Conference room.

Bottom left: Reception and bank tellers.

Opposite above left: Conference/living room lounge area.

Opposite above right: Private offices.

Photography: Jeffrey Jacobs.

RTKL Associates Inc.

CoStar Group
White Marsh, Maryland

It takes bright, ambitious and cooperative people to staff CoStar Group, one of the leading information services for commercial real estate professionals in the United States and the United Kingdom. So when CoStar retained RTKL Associates to help develop a new work environment for 190 employees in a two-floor, 30,000-square-foot space in White Marsh, Maryland, the firm specifically requested a design solution that would address significant turnover by enlivening the workplace, introducing opportunities for personal interaction, and creating the "buzz" its existing cubicles lacked. The resulting facility, comprising private offices, open workstations, training room, video/teleconference room, lunchroom and server room, opens up CoStar in numerous, employee-friendly ways. Private offices have relinquished the perimeter for glass enclosures in the interior, letting everyone share natural light and views while allowing managers to enjoy maximum visibility to their teams. Simultaneously, open workstations have been energized by shifting from a 90-degree grid to a 120-degree one, lowering panel heights, forming team configurations, and embracing brighter color schemes, thanks to contemporary office furnishings chosen for their utility, flexibility and visual excitement, and task and accent lighting that combines sophisticated design with energy conservation. To quote management's comment on the transformation: "White Marsh is awesome."

Above left: Director's office.
Above right: Main conference room.
Right: Conference room.
Below right: Open plan area.
Opposite: Entry lobby and reception.
Photography: Paul Warchol.

RTKL Associates Inc.

American Trucking Associations
Arlington, Virginia

As the American Trucking Associations, the nation's largest national trade association for the trucking industry and a federation of other trucking groups, proudly declares, America's freight moves on trucks. The statistics tell a convincing story. Trucking accounted for 10.7 billion tons of freight or 69 percent of total U.S. freight tonnage in 2006, constituting a $645.6-billion industry or 83.8 percent of the nation's freight bill. An economic powerhouse like this could easily be expected to house itself in a showcase of its members' capabilities, and the new, five-story, 101,000-square-foot headquarters, in Arlington, Virginia, designed by RTKL Associates, does so with considerable skill and artistry. Instead of emphasizing the brute strength of men and machinery, however, the design constructs a branded environment for the ATA founded on the swift and accurate movement of goods, producing a spacious, light and airy setting for 250 employees working in reception areas, private offices, open workstations, conference centers, board room, training room and lunch room. Interestingly, the new headquarters also models its four consecutive floors, the 2nd through 5th floors, and separate 12th floor suite to recreate the visual power of its former premises. By partially removing the third floor, the design opens up a two-story atrium that replicates the sense of arrival evoked by the base building lobby

Top: Lunchroom.
Above: Special functions room.
Left: Atrium lobby.
Opposite: Monumental stair.
Photography: Paul Warchol.

RTKL Associates Inc.

atrium at its previous location. The atrium affords an abundance of natural light and maximizes visibility, giving the ATA a feeling of ownership in its new location as well as a feature to distinguish itself from other tenants in its suburban Washington office building. Extending this imagery throughout the space, the design draws upon such materials as stone, metal, wood, glass and carpet, the brilliant colors of the open road, clean, contemporary furnishings and a nuanced lighting scheme to make architecture seem anything but stationary.

STAFFELBACH

2525 McKinnon Street, Suite 800 • Dallas, TX 75201-1511 • 214.747.2511 • 214.855.5316 (F)

www.staffelbach.com

STAFFELBACH

Urban Towers
Irving, Texas

Left: Entry doorway.

Lower left: Forecourt to entry.

Opposite: Corridor to entry lobby.

Overleaf: Entry lobby with reception and concierge desks.

Photography: Craig Kuhner.

Corporate executives who admit knowing little about architecture and interior design are often surprisingly perceptive about their offices—as well as those of customers, vendors and competitors. Where we work speaks volumes about who we are, so "location, location, location" remains essential to business strategy even in the global economy. CB Richard Ellis Investors, Strategic Partners has made good use of this fact in the award-winning renovation of the Urban Towers, twin Class A office buildings encompassing 835,000 square feet on 39 floors at the fabled Las Colinas district in Irving, Texas, designed by STAFFELBACH. In the drive to create a new entry with a compelling sense of arrival, add vitality and interest to public spaces, reposition the property for increased leasing activity, recapture space for leasing purposes, and update the existing public image or "curb appeal," STAFFELBACH has shrewdly introduced a sleek, contemporary five-star hotel environment along with such five-star amenities as a conference center, fitness center, delicatessen and management offices. Timeless, natural materials and classic furnishings are combined with clean, contemporary architecture to project a look of quality, durability and sustainability, transforming 22 West Las Colinas Boulevard into the latest word on modernity, clarity, style and world-class service.

STAFFELBACH

The Tower on Lake Carolyn
Irving, Texas

How can selected office buildings lead multiple charmed lives as Class A properties, defying the inevitable onset of age, deterioration and obsolescence? Consider the fate of the Tower on Lake Carolyn, in Irving, Texas. The successful renovation of this 19-story, 364,000-square-foot office building, designed by STAFFELBACH for CB Richard Ellis Investors, Strategic Partners, has been constructed on the solid fundamentals of a property with a sound structure, versatile footprint and adaptable infrastructure, characteristics that architects and builders liken to "good bones." Thanks to the extensive makeover, which has established one logical point of arrival and entry, reclaimed leasable space, introduced the conference center and concierge, refurbished the fitness and delicatessen areas, modernized and updated the

property's image, enhanced existing materials with new ones, and endeavored overall to "keep what is good and relevant—and add new where important," the building now boasts a five-star ambiance to match its five-star amenities. Yet the road to the sophisticated new environment was anything but formulaic. STAFFELBACH's design team began the rebranding of the Tower on Lake Carolyn in the same way it launches other design projects, by understanding what the client, CB Richard Ellis Investors, Strategic Partners, sought to achieve. Asking the basic questions that form the foundation of all good project programming (Who are you? What do you do? Why are you

Top: Lobby seating.

Above: View of lobby with ceiling sculpture.

Left: Passage to parking garage.

Opposite: Lobby looking towards main entrance.

Photography: Craig Kuhner.

noteworthy?), the design firm determined exactly what the client required to catapult the aging facility into the ranks of new Class A office buildings in its market territory. Thus, the cool, contemporary interiors have embraced a simple, neutral color palette, timeless natural materials such as stone, wood and glass,

minimally detailed modern furnishings, attractive yet energy-efficient lighting, and easily navigable spatial organization, while allowing for such visual flourishes as a suspended ceiling sculpture of rippling sheet metal that appears to hover effortlessly above the lobby seating areas. Equally important, the project has met its financial

and scheduling goals, remaining fully accessible and operational to tenants during construction and attaining full occupancy later. STAFFELBACH's comprehensive and inspired effort prompted Michael Burrichter, a principal of CB Richard Ellis Investors, Strategic Partners, to tell the *Dallas Business Journal*,

"In today's market, you're bidding against so many others, and the winner is simply the one who submits the high bid. It's all about seeing potential in the property that the other guy doesn't see. André (Staffelbach) can see things that nobody else can. He is truly an artist."

Above: Delicatessen overlooking Lake Carolyn.

Photography: Craig Kuhner.

Ted Moudis Associates

79 Madison Avenue • New York, NY 10016 • 212.308.4000 • 212.561.2020 (F)

One Financial Place • 440 South LaSalle Street • Chicago, IL 60605 • 312.924.5000 • 312.924.5050 (F)

www.tedmoudis.com

Ted Moudis Associates

Coty Inc.
New York, New York

Sarah Jessica Parker, Jennifer Lopez and Celine Dion are just a few of the celebrities who help to make Coty the world's largest fragrance company and a recognized leader in global beauty. Founded in France in 1904 and established in the Americas in 1922, Coty occupies a striking new, 260-person, two-floor, 75,000-square foot office in New York. Designed by Ted Moudis Associates, the new space complements its people and products and enhances the Coty brand. The design's flexibility supports large and small gatherings, casual interaction, and a residential-style atmosphere combining efficiency, comfort and style. Its components, comprising an elevator lobby, reception area, waiting area, private offices, boardroom, open plan workstations, company store, conference/meeting rooms, main pantry café and executive pantry, make creative use of its standard configuration. To maximize daylight and

encourage an open feeling, perimeter-based private offices have full-height glass fronts and workstation partitions are kept low. The café encourages employees' interaction through banquettes and casual tables. In addition, special details, such as a waiting area with an electric fireplace, movable wall units that expand the boardroom for town hall meetings, and contrasting materials such as bamboo floors and a metal-and-glass interconnecting stair, ensure Coty a suitably fashionable workplace.

Top right: Interconnecting stair.

Right: Café.

Lower right: Open plan work-stations and private offices.

Bottom right: Boardroom.

Below: Meeting room.

Below left: Waiting area with fireplace.

Photography: Eric Laignel.

Ted Moudis Associates

Financial Services Firm
New York, New York

When Ted Moudis Associates was recently retained to design a 13,500-square-foot New York office for a 32-person financial services firm, the client's request for a contemporary workplace took an unconventional turn. The new interior would combine the building's panoramic views of midtown Manhattan with materials and colors inspired by the "Big Sky Country" of Montana, a place with strong personal associations for the firm's progressive founder and his family. The Western

influences add unexpected charm to the open and accessible environment. Though the compact floor plan is conventional, comprising of an elevator lobby, reception/ waiting area, private offices, open plan workstations, conference rooms, breakout spaces, support areas, lounge, kitchen, gymnasium and locker rooms, its detailing is not. For example, the reception area and adjacent conference rooms are framed in clear glass, as are all private offices and the rarely

closed double doors to the president's office. The visibility is ideal for displaying outdoor views and such special design features as the sandblasted limestone lobby wall, the tigerskin travertine reception desk, the residential-style pendant light fixture above waiting area seating, and the staff lounge, a comfortable staff "get-away" that accommodates casual meetings. It's "Big Sky Country"—with the Empire State Building on the horizon.

Above: Reception.

Top right: Reception seating.

Right: Large and small conference rooms with reception seating in between.

Lower right: Private offices.

Bottom right: Skyline view.

Opposite: Guest lounge.

Photography: Adrian Wilson.

Ted Moudis Associates

Hunter Roberts Interiors
New York, New York

Hunter Roberts, a respected construction management firm, has opened a midtown Manhattan office for its new Hunter Roberts Interiors division, using the open and dynamic environment to establish the firm as a competitive force within the industry and to help recruit talent. The compact, 10,000-square-foot space, designed by Ted Moudis Associates, includes 30 in-house staff positions with touchdown locations and desks for field supervisors. Its highly functional yet stylish contemporary design demonstrates the organiza-tion's ability to coordinate multiple building trades in delivering a high quality end product within a tight budget and fast timetable. Among its varied facilities are a reception and waiting area, executive boardroom, perimeter and interior private offices, marketing and finance suites, open plan positions for operations and estimating teams, production area, a plan room/area for subcontractors, a pantry and restrooms. The use of metal, glass and wood office fronts, open ceilings and exposed beams and ductwork promotes openness, light and increased collaboration at the same time it reflects a profound commitment to the construction industry. Conse-quently, clients, subcontrac-tors, and field supervisors feel as welcome here as in-house employees, giving Hunter Roberts Interiors an auspicious head start in business.

Below left: Executive board-room.

Below right: Main reception.

Opposite upper left: Office fronts.

Opposite upper center Touchdown locations for field employees.

Opposite upper right: Pantry and lunchroom.

Photography: Adrian Wilson.

Ted Moudis Associates

Investment Management Firm
New York, New York

Top: Reception seating.
Upper left: Private offices.
Upper right: Reception.

Center left: Executive board-room.
Above: Open workstations.
Photography: Peter Paige.

Some 60 employees of a young and dynamic investment management firm have the best of two worlds in their new 16,000-square foot office, designed by Ted Moudis Associates, at New York's prestigious Seagram Building. The facility provides an elegant, modern workplace uniquely suited to the firm's leadership, staff and operations—at the same time it honors the building's historic International Style. What enabled the design to capture the personalities and tastes of the firm's two founding partners was their willingness to participate in design development, considering the forms, materials, furnishings and lighting needed to create a timeless and sophisticated space with flexibility for future growth. The scheme imposes no obtrusive visual barriers between such accommodations as the reception/guest waiting area, executive boardroom, executive lounge, executive offices, perimeter private offices, open workstations, conference rooms, trading suite and pantry. Interior detailing is similarly spare and uncomplicated, from minimally detailed casegoods and seating that contrasts simple lines with rich upholsteries and textured leathers to private offices with full height/seamless glass fronts and doors. And by incorporating the building's signature elements, including its distinctive luminous ceiling, the design links the vision of the firm and its founders to an icon of the corporate world.

Tobin + Parnes Design Enterprises

304 Hudson Street, Suite 500 • New York, NY 10013-1015 • 212.462.4200 • 212.462.4788 (F)

www.tobinparnes.com

Tobin + Parnes Design Enterprises

Mazama Capital Management
New York, New York

If the serenity of Oregon's Willamette Valley flourishes in the New York office of Mazama Capital Management, it's unsurprising to employees and clients of the Oregon-based investment advisory firm. Mazama was founded in Portland in 1993 on the principle that "People Make the Difference." That's why the new one-floor, 5,000-square-foot space, designed for 13 employees by Tobin + Parnes Design Enterprises, is located in the iconic Seagram Building. Yet it also explains why the uniquely beautiful interiors honor

Mazama's Oregon roots. The firm believes outstanding workplaces help attract and retain gifted professionals who consistently deliver top quality service to clients. Developing Mazama's facility has involved preserving the building's historic integrity, incorporating its original illuminated ceiling into the overall design, emphasizing its functionalist aesthetic, and maintaining its emphasis on open plans, natural light, clean lines and rich materials. At the same time, the project has provided the opportunity to construct a user-friendly

setting with subtle references to nature using new and unique materials, such as textural cast plaster panels and translucent acrylic dividing screens. Comments Ron Sauer, Mazama CEO, "The overall design mimics the natural beauty found in Oregon while creating a space where employees and clients can relate and communicate."

Tobin + Parnes Design Enterprises

Tobin + Parnes Design Enterprises
New York, New York

Tobin + Parnes Design Enterprises knows how clients feel. After years of growth, the full-service architectural and interior design firm established by Carol Tobin and Robert Mark Parnes in 1983 recently became its own client to develop a new, 25-person, one-floor, 5,000-square-foot office in lower Manhattan. As in any design project, Tobin + Parnes established its programmatic needs and developed a design solution that responded in a functional, cost-effective, sustainable and aesthetically pleasing way. But the firm didn't stop there, exploring major issues faced by clients. The result is a compelling demonstration of its core design principles. For example, Tobin + Parnes minimized costs and reduced the carbon footprint by reusing existing architectural elements and orienting design studios to harvest daylight instead of overhead lighting. It also applied cost segregation design strategies to optimize accelerated depreciation and maximize tax benefits for construction. Equally important, it turned a raw loft space into an empowering environment. The contemporary design of the reception area, private offices, design studios, conference rooms, library, copy room, pantry, server room and storage, balances privacy with openness and stimulates collaboration. Fresh organic colors, natural materials and sophisticated lighting complete the firm's vision of progressive, sustainable and comprehensive design.

Above left: Passage from reception to design studio.
Left: Office entry.
Below: Design studio.
Opposite: Reception area.
Photography: Ruggero Vanni/ Vanni Archive.

Tobin + Parnes Design Enterprises

S.USA Life Insurance - Sales & Marketing Office
Chicago, Illinois

Constructing a work environment capable of fostering creativity and encouraging open staff interaction and communication may sound like a dream to many organizations. However, S.USA Life Insurance Company, Inc., a wholly-owned subsidiary of SBLI USA Mutual Life Insurance Company, Inc., offers solid evidence that this dream can come true. A new, one-floor, 15,000-square-foot sales and marketing office for 40 S.USA employees in Chicago, designed by Tobin + Parnes Design Enterprises, is providing strong support for the company's expanding national presence with a facility that embodies its energetic spirit and humanistic mission. Standing

conventional office planning on its head, the design scheme places private offices in the interior of the floor and surrounds them with glass to make their occupants visible and accessible while offering daylight and outdoor views to all employees, regardless of rank or title. Correspondingly, staff areas are located near the perimeter walls, where their open workstations enjoy direct exposure to daylight and outdoor views that penetrate deep into the interior space. To keep the facility easy to navigate, serpentine transition spaces announce their presence with the S.USA logo and colorful ceiling and lighting details. Flexibility is accommodated as well with a variety of adaptable spaces that are

Top right: Conference rooms in open configuration.

Above: Main corridor showing soffit detail and art niches.

Left: Reception with operable curved glass wall.

Opposite: Main corridor showing soffit detail.

Photography: Ruggero Vanni/ Vanni Archive.

Tobin + Parnes Design Enterprises

conveniently distributed across the floor to support all manner of needs. Like the activities they support, these spaces range in complexity from walls of curved glass and acoustical operable walls to multi-use conference rooms, a meditation lounge,

breakout space, and casual seating areas. S.USA, a financial services company that is committed to serving the value-conscious consumer, now has a facility that creates comparable value for its occupants as a matter of course—and

appears to be having an effortless and enjoyable time doing it.

Above: Interior offices and open workstation area.

Above left: Executive conference room.

Bottom: Executive office.

VOA Associates Incorporated

224 South Michigan Avenue, Suite 1400 • Chicago, Illinois 60604 • 312.554.1400 • 312.554.1412 (F)

Dubai • Highland, IN • Orlando • São Paulo • Seattle • Washington DC

www.voa.com

VOA Associates Incorporated

RMB Capital Management LLC
Chicago, Illinois

Introduce a successful investment advisor, providing asset management and financial advisory services for individual and institutional investors since 2005, to a high floor of a classic Chicago mid-century office tower, characterized by the clean lines and progressive viewpoint of the International Style, and what can you achieve? For RMB Capital Management, the new, one-floor, 17,000-square-foot office, designed for 65 employees by VOA Associates Incorporated, has emerged as a sleek yet unexpectedly inviting environment. The award-winning space blends RMB's branding scheme, providing investment expertise with the depth of personal service only an independent firm can deliver, and

Right: Café and lounge.

Far right: Reception and conference room.

Below: Elevator lobby and reception.

Opposite above right: Branding boulevard outside the conference area.

Photography: Nick Merrick/ Hedrich Blessing.

the historic essence of the building. What distinguishes the sophisticated setting is its use of unconventional elements of home design, including bookshelves, nature-themed art and built-in planters with thriving greenery. As a result, a basic floor plan of private offices, open workstations, a conference area adjacent to reception, and a café is interpreted in Bubinga wood and other high-end finishes, carpet, skyline glass, and modern furniture to frame spectacular outdoor views of Chicago and Lake Michigan that are shared by the entire staff, making a modern, professional environment comfortable and relaxing as well.

VOA Associates Incorporated

Doane Pet Care
Brentwood, Tennessee

A pet-friendly, outdoor park atmosphere is flourishing inside a modern office where it could not be more appropriate: the headquarters of Doane Pet Care, a two-floor, 66,000-square-foot facility in Brentwood, Tennessee, a leading manufacturer of dry pet food, pet snacks and treats. The facility's mission was straightforward enough. Doane sought to assemble various pet care product groups under one roof to stimulate and support them, turning to VOA Associates Incorporated to design an active and playful workplace that exemplified who they are and what they do. Faced with a tight budget, the design team imaginatively employed colors, shapes and lighting to evoke a park inside the largely open environment of public areas, support spaces, conference rooms, interactive areas and private areas. For example, while a walking path defined by tree trunks, gravel and fire hydrants leads people through the space, the main reception features a broad graphic wall featuring a boxer puppy's face, bright red woven plywood space dividers suggest outdoor fences, and informal furnishings keep rooms cheerful and adaptable. Not only are employees encouraged by the new facility, many more have been inspired to join the Doane family—with their pets, of course.

VOA Associates Incorporated

Leo Burnett USA
Chicago, Illinois

If getting creative people in one of the world's largest and most respected advertising agencies to interact like employees in an edgy, start-up enterprise—and to accomplish this in a space that condenses three floors down to two while providing openness, flexibility, storage and easily identified delineations between separate project teams—sounds daunting, it's time to visit the recently completed, 270-person, two-floor, 50,000-square-foot renovation at Leo Burnett in Chicago. Designed by VOA Associates Incorporated, the space embodies Leo Burnett's workplace vision of creativity, featuring a warehouse atmosphere of open floors, workstations that are compact, mobile and adaptable, modular storage bins with tackable surfaces, adjustable lighting fixtures, vivid colors and utilitarian building materials. VOA designed "billboards" with plywood, cork and metal surfaces that divided workstations into neighborhoods and provided display space. Conceived to

Above right: Workstations at the "billboards."

Right: Main entry at reception.

Opposite: Convertible workspace at the window wall.

Photography: Nick Merrick/ Hedrich Blessing.

VOA Associates Incorporated

encourage the transition from the old button-down image to a new, do-it-yourself vibe, the new workplace is a highly functional facility for displaying work in progress and developing finished art in the process of creating advertising campaigns. Its density has been raised by reducing the amount of private spaces. Yet the floors feel spacious and varied because individual workstations are relatively open, easily customized and frequently reconfigured to express the character of their occupants and project teams, and the expanses they occupy are interspersed with open meeting areas and enclosed teaming and conference rooms. The transformed facility makes a formal nod to its corporate identity at the entrance through its green, white and charcoal styling, which reflects company branding. Yet the presence of the "energy room," a multi-functional break/game/meeting room where employees can re-energize, unwind and challenge each other at foosball, and the presence of employee scooters, provided to help the staff zip through the office, help keep the spirit of Leo Burnett, a former reporter and copywriter who founded his eponymous agency in 1935, alive, healthy and conspicuously zippy. While Burnett's colleagues will never know how the founder might have responded to the space, the AIA Chicago chapter has granted it an Interior Architecture Award for Design Excellence.

Above: Energy room.

Right: View from the energy room into the innovation zone.

Wolcott Architecture Interiors

Wolcott Architecture Interiors

REELZ Channel
Los Angeles, California

Few of us know or care about the workplaces of the broadcast, cable, satellite or Internet services whose programs we watch. Yet the new and inviting, one-floor, 24,500-square-foot Los Angeles office for the 200 employees of REELZ Chan-nel, designed by Wolcott Architecture Interiors, demonstrates that the off-camera environment matters to the media industry. REELZ Channel, a recently launched multi-media brand offering the only cable/satellite TV network and broadband Website dedicated to "Every-thing About Movies, 24/7," wanted a space combining a comfortable and distinctly playful residential aesthetic with cost-effective materials and construction. The project recognizes the long hours employees spend in editing

Above: Branding/logo in reception.

Right: Open work area.

Opposite: Reception.

Photography: Marshal Safron.

and filming while adhering to a modest construction budget. Key to the design are the splashes of color and wood accenting a cozy setting of private offices, open workstations, conference rooms and specialized facilities. The design integrates predominantly neutral tones with drywall, carpet, exposed ceiling, contemporary office furnishings and both direct and indirect lighting. In addition, a collaborative café counter at the center of the space, promotes impromptu brainstorming sessions and other gatherings. A visualization of the company logo in the lobby reinforces the REELZ Channel brand, and adds appropriate, behind-the-scenes drama to a business devoted to movies.

Wolcott Architecture Interiors

Colliers International
Los Angeles, California

Envisioned as unpretentious, low-key and sensible, the integration of existing perimeter offices and new construction has ultimately succeeded for the new Los Angeles office of Colliers International, designed by Wolcott Architecture Interiors. What energizes the new, two-floor, 32,000-square-foot facility for 140 employees of the worldwide affiliation of independently owned and operated commercial real estate businesses, is the inspired use of glass, along with stone, stainless steel, drywall, wallcovering, paint and a sophisticated lighting installation. The impact of glass is everywhere, transmitting natural light and outdoor views deep into the space and creating an aura for such spaces as the reception lobby, boardroom, private offices and open workstations. Space and light appear to flow everywhere, from the interior stair, introduced to stimulate employee interaction, and the adjacent boardroom, which shares a glass wall and a panorama of downtown Los Angeles (overlooking the new L.A. Live and Staples Center) with the reception area, to the team offices, developed to support a more collaborative office culture. Not only has the new facility eliminated the "front and back of house"

demarcation that characterized the company's previous
location, brokers proclaim
that it has "raised our image
to a higher level."

Top left: Visitors lounge.

Top right: Client/employee
informal seating.

Above: Boardroom.

Left: Interior stair.

Opposite: Reception.

Photography: Marshal Safron.

Wolcott Architecture Interiors

Volkswagen/Audi Design Center of California
Santa Monica, California

Top: Modeling studio.
Above: Main conference room.
Opposite: Three-story entry.
Photography: Erhard Pfeiffer.

"What do you drive?" The question is as essential to everyday California life as freeways, which helps explain why major carmakers maintain design studios in southern California, ready to catch the next wave in motoring trends. The presence of Art Center College, the prominent school of industrial design in Pasadena, is another inducement. The Golden State's passion for the road is memorably captured in the new Volkswagen/Audi Design Center of California, a three-story, 50,000-square-foot facility in Santa Monica, designed by Wolcott Architecture Interiors. The Center occupies the former Museum of Flying, located adjacent to Santa Monica Airport, adapting an exposed steel frame structure that once displayed historic aircraft and exhibitions on flight to house separate studios for Volkswagen of America's two fabled brands, Volkswagen and Audi. Every detail of the existing structure, including its soaring three-story atrium, is carefully considered in the new scheme. For example, the ground floor's ample floor area and high ceiling

Wolcott Architecture Interiors

let design studios' modeling departments spread out and view concept cars from every angle, aided by a state-of-the-art fluorescent strip light system that is easily accommodated by the high ceiling, and a common workshop facility located between each studio that accomodates high-tech tools and equipment. On the second floor, the design staff works in an open environment featuring workstations that encourage team collaboration and afford designers a bird's eye view of clay models on the floor below. The stacking plan concludes with the public reception area, main conference center, executive designer offices and employee lunchroom on the third floor. Because of the growing importance of design to the automotive industry, the Center is as sensitive to sight lines and lighting as it is to space and form. In addition to capping the atrium with a signature pyramid of light-weight framing and translucent panels, offering the modeling area visual security while establishing a glowing lantern at night, the design restores the existing glass clerestory throughout the building to provide daylight for all employees. The Center ensures that winning designs for future Volkswagens and Audis will always be seen in their best light.

Top: Design studio.

Above: Reception lobby.

Left: Seating area and conference room.

Zimmer Gunsul Frasca Architects LLP

320 SW Oak Street, Suite 500 • Portland, OR 97204 • 503.224.3860 • 503.224.2482 (F)

1350 Avenue of the Americas, Suite 820 • New York, NY 10019 • 212.624.4754 • 212.624.4753 (F)

925 Fourth Avenue, Suite 2400 • Seattle, WA 98104 • 206.623.9414 • 206.623.7868 (F)

515 South Flower Street, Suite 3700 • Los Angeles, CA 90071 • 213.617.1901 • 213.617.0047 (F)

1800 K Street NW, Suite 200 • Washington, DC 20006 • 202.380.3120 • 202.380.3128 (F)

www.zgf.com

Zimmer Gunsul Frasca Architects LLP

University of Arizona
Thomas W. Keating Bioresearch Building/Medical Research Building
Tucson, Arizona

Left: Corridor.
Below: Conference room.
Bottom: Café.
Opposite: Stair.
Photography: Robert Canfield.

Developing extraordinary workplaces for top scientists is almost mandatory when you're a leading public research university in the Southwest. Consider two new research facilities designed by Zimmer Gunsul Frasca Architects for the University of Arizona in Tucson: the four-story, 177,063-square-foot Thomas W. Keating Bioresearch Building and four-story, 143,257-square-foot Medical Research Building. Besides providing modern laboratories, the linked structures encourage interaction and sharing among faculty and students from the Colleges of Science, Agriculture and Life Sciences, Medicine, Pharmacy and Engineering and Mines in the Keating Building, a boxy mass flanked by laboratories forming an L to the south and east; and basic scientists

and physician researchers in the MRB, a rectangular mass to the north with north-facing laboratories and south-facing offices. Not only can researchers work in flexible, interdisciplinary laboratories, laboratory support spaces, faculty offices and open-plan graduate student workstations, they can meet in such attractive social spaces as conference rooms, break rooms, atrium, lobbies and stairs. There are four connecting elements, including a below-grade vivarium, ground-level ramada, second-level open exterior bridge and third- and fourth-level enclosed bridge containing office space. Robert Smith, University Director, Facilities Design and Construction, says, "These new facilities represent a bold, innovative addition to our campus."

Zimmer Gunsul Frasca Architects LLP

Microsoft Corporation
Building 88
Redmond, Washington

What could easily have been the conventional renovation of an existing office building at Microsoft Corporation's campus in Redmond, Washington, has been revealed as considerably more interesting. Since the global software giant relies on the recruitment and retention of brilliant employees to maintain its competitive stance, it has conducted a three-year initiative to research its workers' space needs, called Global Workplace Strategies, to develop workplace environments that are highly desirable to recruits, embody innovation and sustainability, and value employees' health. Building 88, a three-level, 217,000-square-foot facility comprising a two-story central atrium, 750 private offices and a generous variety of meeting spaces, has been designed by Zimmer Gunsul Frasca Architects to incorporate the findings of GWS. These goals include maintaining private spaces yet dissolving barriers between individual modules, creating team settings that encourage collaboration, and supporting mobile, tech-savvy workers with open touchdown workspaces. The LEED CI Gold-certified design encourages active discussion between colleagues wherever and whenever it occurs. Such venues as translucent individual offices, fully wired informal meeting spaces, strategically located teaming areas with work tables, tack surfaces, white boards, daylight and views, and large "think tanks" directly connected to kitchenettes make being young, bright and ambitious look very appealing indeed.

Top right: Interior private offices.

Above right: Perimeter support and interaction space.

Above left: Touchdown stations.

Left: Entrance lobby.

Opposite: Informal meeting area.

Photography: Eckert & Eckert.

Zimmer Gunsul Frasca Architects LLP

The Children's Hospital
Denver, Colorado

Founded in 1908, The Children's Hospital in Denver is considered one of the best of its kind by *U.S. News & World Report*. So when the hospital began developing its new, 270-bed, nine-floor, 1.44 million-square-foot replacement hospital, designed by Zimmer Gunsul Frasca Architects, it demanded a "most healing hospital" revolving around family-centered care, reflecting best practices, and incorporating evidence-based design. The benefits of this approach are visible everywhere, from the Boettcher Atrium, the hospital's daylight-filled "public living room," to the "hybrid" inpatient nursing units coupling centralized caregivers "hubs" with decentralized charting

stations; patient rooms offering patient, caregiver and family "zones;" and such family amenities as a family lounge, family laundry and family sleep rooms. Besides visiting and benchmarking a dozen children's hospitals, conducting patient/family and community focus groups, and studying evidence-based design, a team of seven designers spent two intensive weeks shadowing and interviewing patients, families and over 250 hospital staff members. How successful is the outcome? Patients and their family members are reporting greater satisfaction in seven categories of service, including the appearance of the patient rooms, accommodations and comfort for visitors, comfort of overnight facilities, and

cheerfulness of the hospital. The hospital has also seen an increase in visitors and improvement in staff retention and recruiting.

Top left: Outpatient pavilion.

Top right to bottom: Patient room; centralized nursing station; chapel; cafeteria; gelato bar.

Opposite: Boettcher Atrium.

Photography: Eckert & Eckert; Basil Childers

Zimmer Gunsul Frasca Architects LLP

University of Oregon
Athletic Medicine Center
Eugene, Oregon

Sports was probably a vital aspect of student life at the University of Oregon, a world-class teaching and research university in Eugene founded in 1876, long before the first football game was held (1894) and the first track team was organized (1895). Today, the new, one-floor, 15,000-square-foot Athletic Medicine Center, designed by Zimmer Gunsul Frasca Architects, continues the legacy by bringing a state-of-the-art sports therapy and training facility for over 400 student-athletes to the school's Casanova Center. It is a sleek, modern, high-tech environment of glass, wood and ceramic tile on an L-shaped floor plan, where three larger spaces for massage, taping, hot/cold pools and hydrotherapy are bordered by a reception and seating area, X-ray facility, nutrition bar, conference and meeting rooms, and treatment rooms featuring treadmills and exercise bikes, vibration platforms, examination rooms for a dentist, ophthalmologist and acupuncturist as well as five additional medical examination rooms. Practical as the award-winning facility is, it also showcases Oregon's athletic history and brands its athletic program without detracting from its Spartan elegance. If anything, the design has made Oregon's search for a holistic approach to student-athletes' health, addressing healing, strength building, nutrition and wellness, worth waiting for.

Top left: Nutrition bar.
Top right: Conference room.
Above: Massage/taping.
Far left: Optical display surrounding nutrition bar.
Left: Hot/cold pools.
Photography: Basil Childers.

Design with light.™

WELCOME TO THE REALITY-BASED OFFICE

By Roger Yee

Corporate America is engaging the global economy with growing pragmatism, creativity and urgency—and reshaping the office for a distinctly 21st-century way of working

Is what's good for General Motors still good for America? The answer isn't as clear as it was to Charles E. Wilson, president of General Motors and future Secretary of Defense under Dwight D. Eisenhower when he made his famous declaration during Senate confirmation hearings in 1953. As Americans have discovered, U.S. companies are competing in a global economy where success does not always require American employees, vendors or customers. It's not unthinkable that Chrysler, desperate for new products but short on cash, may rebrand Nissans to fill its lines. Or that IBM's 53,000-strong work force in India will soon progress from product design and development to product conceptualization. Or that America's mightiest financial institutions may be controlled by overseas entities, a genuine possibility given such recent transactions as the bankruptcy of Lehman Brothers, which led Barclays and Nomura to acquire its operations, one of many unprecedented events in the Wall Street crash of September 2008.

Where this leaves American workers is unclear. Whereas many European and Asian nations practice mercantilist or fair trade capitalism, favoring local employment and control of key business assets, the United States champions laissez-faire or free trade capitalism, putting American jobs and other vital resources into play whenever better deals are available. The shipping of entire factories from our shores to Asia, Eastern Europe or South America to slash labor costs can bring cheers to shareholders and tears to workers.

"Offshoring" lets American consumers buy more goods for less money, but its cost goes beyond lost jobs. Persistent U.S. deficits in global trade, coupled with chronic government reliance on debt, have degraded the dollar and rattled world financial markets. As good as the cheap dollar has been for the nation's exports, it has turned such corporate icons as Anheuser-Busch, GE Plastics, Genentech and John Hancock into bargains for overseas buyers.

Above: Attractive and accessible conference facilities and common areas at Nuvera Fuel Cells, in Billerica, Massachusetts, help unite a diverse work force distributed among offices and laboratories.

Better. Faster. Greener.

You know you can rely on Grand Rapids Chair for superior quality, durability and speed. But did you know our tables and chairs offer significant environmental advantages, as well? We use certified renewable wood. Recycled steel. No-VOC paints. And a whole host of other green materials and techniques that can help you earn LEED certification. Visit our web site to learn more!

GRAND RAPIDS CHAIR COMPANY®

Made Green in the USA

www.grandrapidschair.com or 1.866.4LEGS4U

If anything, American workers have contributed to the resiliency of the U.S. economy despite near-recessionary conditions. Consider that unit labor cost in the United States increased by just 1.5 percent through the second quarter of 2008 while productivity rose by 2.8 percent. Because of key changes in corporate labor policy—such as the growing use of part-time workers (easy to hire and fire), companies' increasing tendency to reduce hours rather than lay off employees, and restrained hiring that has kept job creation abnormally low—corporate America is keeping labor cost under control even as demand for products falters.

True, the mediocre performance of U.S. students in global comparisons of proficiency in mathematics, reading and science bolsters employers' complaints about the lack of qualified American workers to fill highly skilled and better paid positions. But academic qualification is not the issue when American companies shop abroad for cheaper alternatives to domestic scientists, engineers, lawyers or financial analysts. The stark reality is that the United States is making painful adjustments to bring pay scales and living standards more in line with those in rival economies such as China, India and Russia. That's why U.S. unemployment

Supporting workforce diversity: Is the office really one happy family?

A half-century ago, men and women diligently wore business suits and conservative dresses, white shirts and blouses, formal footwear and hats to look alike. Today, once-suppressed differences of age, sex, ethnicity and social class are more openly expressed by an increasingly diverse population, with mixed results. "Differences in the workforce are becoming more pronounced in some ways and less in others," reports Joseph Flynn, a senior associate of Margulies Perruzzi Architects.

How does generational conflict enter the office? A common problem is that older employees want more light, whereas younger ones want less. "Losses of vision and hearing are noticeable for workers in their 50s," Flynn says. "Compensating

stood at 6.1 percent in August 2008 and the American family's median purchasing power has not advanced significantly since the 1970s.

Since technology, capital and jobs can now travel anywhere at the speed of a keystroke, it makes sense for U.S. employers to give their well educated, highly productive, and decently paid American employees workplaces where they can excel. Fortunately, the nation's leading architects and interior designers serving business report that their clients are doing just that. Corporate executives are turning to design to create offices that support work force diversity, keep workers connected, accommodate multiple work modes, and promote sustainable working environments and work-life balance. As the newest crop of commercial and institutional offices dramatically demonstrates, the design community is enthusiastically confronting these challenges.

for an aging population is altering our view of universal design. The issue is how to create a baseline for people of all physical abilities that goes beyond the ADA (Americans with Disabilities Act)."

Gender preferences also emerge in the office, though Flynn insists they seldom create problems. "Predominately female workplaces are more egalitarian and social," he states. "Male-dominated offices are more team-oriented and hierarchic." As for ethnicity and social class, younger workers are comfortable with multi-cultural backgrounds.

It's hard to change old habits, nonetheless. Younger workers may want spaces that foster more openness, interaction and collaboration, but older workers aren't ready to give up "my office, my staff, my project." "People aren't lab rats," Flynn

Above: This elegant yet comfortable artist room in the executive area of EMI Music Japan, in Tokyo, Japan, is one of many thoughtful meeting spaces where visiting artists feel connected with the company.

GIANNI

ALLIANCE

TRADITIONAL METHODS, CONTEMPORARY SOLUTIONS

From the Boardroom to the General Office
Functional, Elegant, Timeless
Office Furniture in Wood

www.gianniinc.com

4615 W. Roosevelt Rd., Cicero, Il. 60804 Tel.708.863.6696 Fax.708.863.4071
Showroom 10.124 Merchandise Mart - Chicago

reminds designers. "They'll find the niches to do what they need to do whether design provides them or not. If an organization wants to encourage them to respond quickly to changing conditions, it will need workplaces with flexible accommodations. We must plan more for what we don't know."

Keeping workers connected: Can an office unite mobile employees?

*D*o you think of an office as a laboratory for teamwork? "Offices are shifting from head-down to collaborative work," according to Andrew Garnar-Wortzel, a principal of Gensler and practice area leader for consulting at the firm. "An explosion in mobile working among mainstream businesses is transforming the role of the office."

Being mobile can signify being on the road, in the client's office, at home or in the local diner. "Mobility is about being in the office part of the time to interact with colleagues," Garnar-Wortzel explains. "Companies find that people can work as well or better away from their desks, and are giving them the flexibility to do it."

Corporate real estate executives like worker mobility as an opportunity to reduce office space. However, Garnar-Wortzel cautions, companies must rethink management's role to account for workers who are electronically tethered but out of sight. "Many managers are nervous about empty desks," he admits. "They must understand *how* their people perform, rather than *where* and *when*. Not everyone is suited for outside work."

An office designed for mobile workers must function as a gathering place, even as the percentage of desk-bound workers rises. "When much of the workforce is elsewhere, you want high density for vitality and buzz," Garnar-Wortzel notes. "Stripping unnecessary conventional office details and introducing whatever supports collaboration can give a powerful boost to productivity."

He likens the heart of the new workplace to a compact airport lounge with library-style tables and carrels as well as soft seating and coffee tables. However, workers must also reinvent their lives for mobility to succeed. Besides becoming more self-disciplined, Garnar-Wortzel says, they typically burden their homes with shelves, files and desktops.

Accommodating multiple work modes: Why do people in offices work so differently?

*B*usiness people now acknowledge that white-collar personnel— whose work has become progressively more conceptual and less mechanistic— should be free to follow multiple work modes. Office occupants share some essential needs, to be sure. "Research shows that knowledge workers excel with stimulating work environments, physical exercise, and personal control over lighting, temperature, air volume and other physical conditions," states Leigh Stringer, LEED AP, a vice president, Advanced Strategies, of HOK/Hellmuth, Obata & Kassabaum. "But they also work best in different ways. I like a cone of silence around me. You're happy in Starbucks."

Developing office space to support multiple work modes requires more than a menu of spaces for individual and group work. "You've got to train people in the new technologies that let them take work anywhere, and to organize them to use roller cases, backpacks, lockers and other equipment to keep track of their belongings," Stringer points out. "At the same time, you must find the right mix of funky spaces in the right locations to reflect the way people actually work and to minimize conflicts due to noise and commotion. And be prepared to spend more on maintenance as you spend less on walls and doors. Collaboration can be very messy."

Stringer believes that while privacy will always be respected in the office, the long-term design trend will be to encourage interaction and sharing. "Hoarding information is bad when no one has all the answers," she argues. "Office design

Above: Since employees of MediaCom, in Toronto, Canada, do some of their best work away from their desks, the company has provided such spaces as this lively bistro as gregarious alternate work sites.

The Original

EXCLUSIVELY AT OSI FURNITURE
555 SANTA ROSA DR.
DES PLAINES, IL 60018
800-445-WOOD (9663)
WWW.OSIFURNITURE.COM

should provide visual access to your team's area, although your manager need not see you directly. Even lawyers are coming around to greater openness."

Promoting sustainable environments and work-life balance: Can the benefits of green design be measured?

Whether or not former Vice President Al Gore has correctly analyzed global warming, businesses are already developing "green" offices. As Heidi Hendy, a principal of H. Hendy Associates, declares, "Sustainability is now everyone's responsibility. Costs have dropped, removing the premium for green design. So going green doesn't have to cost clients more, making everyone happy."

Hendy reports that 10 percent of clients are deeply committed to the cause, exploring advanced technologies for their projects. Their motives aren't entirely altruistic, of course. "They expect a return on their investments," Hendy reports. "At the same time, they want to improve the world we give to the next generation."

Fortunately, their leaders are part of a growing crusade for sustainable materials, zero off-gassing, clean air, energy and water conservation and other "green" construction goals. Not only are millennials pressing for more social responsibility in business, government is getting involved at the federal level through the General Services Administration, across the State of California, and in municipalities too. For these reasons and more, office workers are routinely

discovering such green and healthy initiatives as fitness equipment, showers, daylight and ergonomic furniture at work.

Companies are likewise endeavoring to develop workplaces that help employees achieve a good work-life balance. Again, altruism mixes here with business. "Work-life issues are often quite basic, like juggling the care of young children and aging parents with the concerns of the job," Hendy indicates. Though companies channel much of their family support through flexible employment policies, on-site facilities such as employee lounges, on-site food and beverage services, lactation rooms, privacy booths, emergency daycare facilities and community rooms can also help lower employee stress. "My clients promote sustainability and healthy living in the office out of respect for their employees," Hendy concludes.

What do American companies want offices to do for their employees in the long run?

So what is today's office, a liability or an asset? "Corporate real estate is not just about cutting costs," says Dennis Gaffney, AIA, LEED AP, a vice president of RTKL Associates. "You spend money where you can get a good return. Businesses know they must do something positive for employees or the 'iPod generation' will walk out."

According to Gaffney, corporate America is learning to link office design with corporate strategy, developing environments that nurture productivity,

Above: Having a dedicated break room for meals is one of numerous ways El Pollo Loco, in Costa Mesa, California, has focused on quality of life for office employees of the growing restaurant chain.

A perfect match.

Dependable service. Exceptional craft.

As the premier resource for architects, designers and facilities professionals, Dfm uses its unique West Coast perspective to create exceptional casegoods, seating and accessories for the contract furniture market. Recognized for creativity and responsiveness since 1927, Dfm delivers finely crafted furniture that fits in perfectly with any corporate environment.

Showroom: 1255 Battery St. Suite 200, San Francisco, CA 94111 [415] 362.5888 dependablefm.com

teamwork and creative thinking. "Business people find that a good office can improve recruitment, morale and retention," he maintains. "However, they have to acknowledge such realities as what the company does for a living and the resources employees need if a design is to succeed."

Branding the office, for example, establishes continuity between the office and the outside world. What the company sells to customers, how it deals with employees, and where it contributes to society are aspects of branding that can be made visible by design. As Gaffney observes, outsiders are not the only people grateful to learn more about the company.

To engage employees fully, the company must be candid about helping them perform at their best. "People still want their own workspaces," Gaffney states. "They also appreciate 'comfort zones' that support alternate work modes, so war rooms, lounges, coffee bars and individual workstations feel equally appropriate as workspaces. In addition, they need home-like private areas to deal with personal matters of finance, family and health."

Major amenities such as gyms, daycare centers and cafeterias are only included if the numbers justify their expense, and often prove more feasible when a landlord offers them to all tenants in an office building or office complex. On the other hand, businesses recognize that face-to-face encounters remain essential for key relationships, and that the office is ideal for staging them. "Executive offices remain a fact of life," Gaffney adds. "But the executive suite is going away so executives can have easier access to their juniors—and vice versa."

"It's not the good old days in business anymore," he sums up. "Workers recognize it, and their offices should too."

Top right: While some organizations seem too complex to understand, the American Trucking Associations, in Arlington, Virginia, celebrates the industry that moves much of America's freight.

Above: Since Gibraltar Bank is a private bank catering to wealthy individuals and families, its New York branch is branded accordingly, with high-end interiors and a view of Park Avenue.

If Walls Could Talk

Walls and ceilings would request Novawall® stretch fabric coverings, the system with sustainable LEED credit attributes.

Novawall® is the industry leader for stretch fabrics used in sustainable interior design. Novawall® uses EcoTRACK, the first PVC-free extrusion process in the industry, and features recycled content core materials as well as fabrics made with renewable/recyclable content.

With Ecogear, Novawall®'s contributions calculator, we'll analyze LEED credit contributions and prepare the paperwork for you, which makes Novawall® the ecologically responsible choice for your project, and the right business choice for you.

NOVAWALL SYSTEMS, INC.
The Standard for Fabric Wall and Ceiling Systems

MEMBER

800.695.6682

sales@novawall.com

www.novawall.com

Resources*

Abu Dhabi Commercial Bank
Design Firm: Gensler
Furniture: B&B Italia, Unifor, Vitra
Carpets & Flooring: Interface
Fabrics: Designtex
Lighting: Erco Lighting
Ceilings: SAS Ceilings
Wallcoverings and Paint: Dulux
Window Treatments: MechoShade
Lighting Consultants: Erco Lighting

Accenture
Design Firm: CBT
Furniture: Andreul World, Bernhardt, Datesweiser, Dunbar, Geravasoni Office Specialty, Keilhauer, Prismatique
Carpets & Flooring: Atlas, Apavista, Dunis Studio, Kentucky Wood Floor, Office Gumar Stone, Shep Brown Associates
Fabrics: Edelman Leather, Elmo Leather, Gretchen Bellinger, Maharam, Quadrant
Lighting: Delray, Flos, Illuminating Experiences, Juno, Kramer, Ledalite, Leucos, Lightolier, Mark Lighting, Portfolio, Vode, Wexer & Ducre, Zaneen
Ceilings: Armstrong
Wallcoverings and Paint: C2 Paint, ICI
Window Treatments: Carnegie, Marjorie Royer Interiors
General Contractors: Shawmut Design & Construction
Lighting Consultants: Sladen Feinstein, Integrated Lighting

Added Value
Design Firm: Gensler
Furniture: Herman Miller, Knoll, Martin Brattrud, Moroso, Ross Lovegrove
Carpets & Flooring: Decorative Carpet, Lumiseal, Milliken
Fabrics: Formica, Momentum
Lighting: Cheryl Townsend
Wallcoverings and Paint: Benjamin Moore
General Contractors: Turner Construction Co.

Analysis Group, Chicago
Design Firm: CBT
Furniture: Bernhardt, Brayton, Brent Comber, Bright, Datesweiser, Davis, Decca, Herman Miller, Keilhauer, Knoll, Neudorfer
Carpets & Flooring: Atlas, Bentley Prince Street, Invision, Mirage Tile, Monterey
Fabrics: Donghia, Luna, Sina Pearson, Spinneybeck
Lighting: Alight, Alkco, Birchwood, Delray, Design

Within Reach, Gotham, Ledalite, Mark Lighting, Metalux
Ceilings: Armstrong, Newmat Luminous Panels
Wallcoverings and Paint: Benjamin Moore, Sherwin-Williams
General Contractors: ICG
Lighting Consultants: Charter Sills

Analysis Group, Inc., New York
Design Firm: CBT
Furniture: Alea, Brent Comber, Datesweiser, Davis Furniture, Decca, Herman Miller, Knoll, Neudorfer
Fabrics: Brentano, Knoll, Kvadrat, Maharam
Lighting: Elliptipar, Kurt Versen, Ledalite, Mark Architectural Lighting, USA Illumination
Ceilings: Armstrong, Barrisol
Wallcoverings and Paint: Benjamin Moore, Designtex, Trove Wallcovering
General Contractors: John Gallin & Son, Inc.
Lighting Consultants: Horton Lees Brogden

ArcLight Capital Partners
Design Firm: CBT
Furniture: Bernhardt, Davis, HBF, Keilhauer, Woodtech
Carpets & Flooring: Karastan, Tura
Fabrics: HBF, Knoll, Maharam, Sina Pearson
Lighting: Belfer, Focal Point, Kurt Versen, Lightolier, Pathway, Studio Design Italia
Ceilings: Armstrong
Wallcoverings and Paint: Armorcoat, Benjamin Moore, Dunon, ICI, Innovations
Window Treatments: MechoShade
General Contractors: Turner, Special Projects Division
Lighting Consultants: Slader Feinstein

CB Richard Ellis, Philadelphia Headquarters
Design Firm: Partridge Architects Inc.
Furniture: Knoll
Carpets & Flooring: Forbo, Johnsonite, Mannington, Shaw Contract
Fabrics: Knoll, Maharam, MDC
Lighting: Artemide, Bruck, Lightolier, Louis Poulsen, Prima Lighting, Tango
Ceilings: Armstrong
Wallcoverings and Paint: Sherwin Williams
General Contractors: D'Lauro & Rodgers

The Children's Hospital
Design Firm: Zimmer Gunsul Frasca Architects LLP
Furniture: Agati, Berco Inc., Brandrud, Brayton, Dauphin, Dellarobbia, Gordon International,

Herman Miller, Keilhauer, Knoll, Landscape Forms, Magnus Olesen A/S, Nemschoff, New World Millworks, NK Medical Poducts, Skeie AS, Sleepcare, Steelcase, Stryker Corp., Swedese Mobler, TotaLibra, Touhy, Weiland
Carpets & Flooring: American Olean, Armstrong, Atlas Carpet, Forbo, Interface, J&J/Invision, Kohler, Lonseal, Pratt & Larson Ceramics, Shaw, Tandus, Tarkett, United Tile
Fabrics: ArcCom, Designtex, Knoll, Maharam, Sina Pearson
Lighting: Genlyte Group, Louis Poulsen, WPT Design, Zumtobel
Ceilings: Ecophon, USG
Wallcoverings and Paint: Carnegie, DuPont, Formica, Forms+Surfaces, ISEC Inc., Rulon, Sherwin-Williams
Window Treatments: MechoShade
General Contractors: GH Phipps Construction Companies and McCarthy Building Companies Inc. joint venture
Lighting Consultants: Francis Krahe & Associates Inc.

Citigroup Shanghai Headquarters
Design Firm: HLW International LLP
Furniture: Haworth, Steelcase, Vanguard
Carpets & Flooring: Armstrong, Interface, Milliken
Lighting: NVC, Philips
Ceilings: Armstrong, Lafarge
Wallcoverings and Paint: Dulux
Window Treatments: Shanghai Qinying
General Contractors: Suzhong Construction Group Co., Ltd., Environetics Design Group International Inc.

Clarins New York Headquarters
Design Firm: Gerner Kronick + Valcarcel, Architects, PC
Furniture: Bernhardt, Datesweiser, Harter, Herman Miller, Knoll, Kresentz Furniture, Nordic Interior, Steelcase
Carpets & Flooring: Johnsonite, Karastan
Lighting: Litecontrol
Ceilings: Armstrong
Wallcoverings and Paint: Benjamin Moore, Maya Romanoff, 3Form, Tri-Kes

Colliers International
Design Firm: Wolcott Architecture Interiors
Furniture: Allsteel, Westfall Commercial Furniture
Carpets & Flooring: Constantine, Invision

*An Incomplete list of major sources.
For more information please call design firms.*

I LIGHT YOU.

Mercury, design Ross Lovegrove

**Professional Lighting Solutions
for Corporate Interiors**

ATLANTA
BOSTON
CHICAGO
DALLAS
DENVER
HONOLULU
LAS VEGAS
LOS ANGELES
MIAMI
MINNEAPOLIS
NEW YORK
PHILADELPHIA
SAN DIEGO
SAN FRANCISCO
SCOTTSDALE
SEATTLE
ST. LOUIS
WASHINGTON D.C.

Artemide

THE HUMAN LIGHT.

1-877-Art-9111 • artemide.us

Fabrics: Bernhardt, Designtex, Knoll
Lighting: Architectural Lighting Axo, Lithonia
Ceilings: Armstrong
Wallcoverings and Paint: Knoll
Window Treatments: MechoShade
General Contractors: Warner

Comerica Bank Headquarters
Design Firm: NELSON
Furniture: Cabot Wrenn, Council Contract, David Edward, Decca, HBF, Kimball, OFS, Steelcase
Carpets & Flooring: Bentley, Constantine, Ergon, Forbo, Global Accents, Kate-Lo, Lees, RBC Tile, Walker Zanger
Fabrics: Architex, Beacon Hill, Brentano, HBF, Robert Allen, Sina Pearson, Textus
Lighting: Alger International, Elliptipar, Justice Design Group, Kurt Versen, Ledalite, Lightolier, Williams
Ceilings: Armstrong
Wallcoverings and Paint: Benjamin Moore, Command, DL Couch, Knoll Textiles, MDC, Scuffmaster, Versa
Window Treatments: MechoShade
General Contractors: Turner Construction
Lighting Consultants: NELSON

CO-OP Financial Services
Design Firm: H. Hendy Associates
Furniture: HBF, Herman Miller, Martin Brattrud, Westcoast Industries, Workplace Resource
Carpets & Flooring: Chilewich, Shaw Contract
Fabrics: HBF, Jhane Barnes
Lighting: Bruck Lighting, Gotham, Litecontrol, Lithonia, Mark Lighting, Peerless, Performance Lighting Systems, Three Form
Ceilings: Armstrong
Wallcoverings and Paint: Koroseal, Zolatone
Window Treatments: Mariak
General Contractors: Accord Electric, Moen Woodworks, Turek
Lighting Consultants: ORESA Partners

Copper Station Holdings
Design Firm: LS3P Associates Ltd.
Furniture: David Edward, HBF, Hudson Furniture, Knoll, Vitra
Carpets & Flooring: Dura Palm Hardwood Floor, Island Stone, Monterey, Rajah Natural Slate, Roppe, Santa Regina Terrazzo Tile, Shaw Carpet
Lighting: Lightolier, Tech Lighting
Ceilings: Armstrong, Ultima Vector
Wallcoverings and Paint: Akdo Glass Wall Tiles, Architex, Benjamin Moore, ICI, Sherwin-Williams
Window Treatments: Lutron Sheer Shade

General Contractors: Hitt Contracting
Lighting Consultants: Chuck Thompson Lighting

Corporate Business Interiors, Inc.
Design Firm: H. Hendy Associates
Furniture: Allsteel, DIRTT, Furniture Solutions, Inc., Gunlocke
Carpets & Flooring: Cheliwich, Habitus Cork, Interface, Spec Ceramics
Fabrics: Allsteel, Brise, Luna, Maharam
Lighting: Cooper, Focal Point, Hampstead, Schmitz, Southern Califormnia Illumination
Wallcoverings and Paint: Carnegie, MDC, Wovin Wall, Zolatone
General Contractors: JLC Associates

Coty, Inc.
Design Firm: Ted Moudis Associates
Furniture: Bernhardt, Brayton, Harter, HBF, Holly Hunt, Steelcase, Touhy
Carpets & Flooring: Allstate, Durkan, Interface, Lees, Natural Cork, Pyramid Flooring, Shag Rug Textiles
Fabrics: Designtex, Luna Textiles, Maharam, Sina Pearson
Lighting: Alko, Atlite, Kurt Versen, Lightolier, Mark Lighting, 3G Lighting
Ceilings: Armstrong, Decoustics
Wallcoverings and Paint: JM Lynne, Knoll, LM Frono Raje, Maharam, Robin Reigi
General Contractors: James G. Kennedy & Co., Inc.

Dechert LLP
Design Firm: HLW International LLP
Furniture: B&B Italia, Bernhardt, Brueton, Datesweiser, Fritz Hansen, Geiger, HBF, Keilhauer, Knoll
Carpets & Flooring: Armstrong, Constantine, Invision, Stone Source
Fabrics: Bernhardt Textiles, Cortine Leather, HBF Textiles, Knoll, Larsen, Maharam, Spinneybeck Leather
Lighting: Edison Price, FineLite, Louis Poulsen, Price Lite, Schmita
Ceilings: Armstrong, Ecophani
Wallcoverings and Paint: Benjamin Moore, Carnegie, Faram, Vivid Products
Window Treatments: Sol-R-Shade
General Contractors: Turner Construction-Special Projects
Lighting Consultants: HLW Internaitonal LLP

Decision One Mortgage - HSBC
Design Firm: LS3P Associates Ltd.
Furniture: Brayton International, Halcon, HBF,

Keilhauer, KI, Metro, Steelcase, Vecta
Carpets & Flooring: Armstrong, Constantine, Crossville, Daltile, Eco Surfaces, Superior Tile
Fabrics: Designtex, Maharam
Lighting: Finelite, Lithonia, Planlicht, RSA, Schmitz Lighting, Shaper
Ceilings: Armstrong
Wallcoverings and Paint: Benjamin Moore, Innovations, JM Lynne, Knoll, Maharam, National Wallcovering, Sherwin-Williams, Xorel
General Contractors: Lauth Property Group
Lighting Consultants: Bodwell & Associates

Dfm
Design Firm: Huntsman Architectural Group
Furniture: Dfm, Eames Aluminum Management Chair, Emeco Barstool
Carpets & Flooring: Junckers, Monterey, Walker Zanger
Lighting: Linear Lighting
Wallcoverings and Paint: Kelly Moore
General Contractors: Peacock Construction

El Pollo Loco Corporate Headquarters
Design Firm: H. Hendy Associates
Furniture: Geiger, Herman Miller, OFS, Valentine Woodworks, West Coast Industries
Carpets & Flooring: Designweave
Fabrics: Architex, Knoll, Paul Brayton
Lighting: Bruck, Focal Point, Leucos, Litecontrol, Prudential
Ceilings: Armstrong
Wallcoverings and Paint: Maharam, Xorel
Window Treatments: Mermet Roller Shades
General Contractors: Casco

EMI Music, Japan
Design Firm: Gensler
Furniture: Aidec, COR, Flitzhansen, Herman Miller, Wilkhan, Yamagiwa, Zanotta
Carpets & Flooring: ABC Ceramics, Advan, Shaw, Toli
Fabrics: Knoll
Lighting: Artemide, Foscarini, Modular, Yamagiwa
Ceilings: Nittobo
Wallcoverings and Paint: Aizu
Window Treatments: Creation Baumann
General Contractors: Obayashi JV

Financial Offices & Call Center
Design Firm: NELSON
Furniture: Bernhardt, Knoll, Steelcase
Carpets & Flooring: Armstrong, Forbo, Italgraniti, Shaw Commercial Carpet, Terrazzo & Marble, Walker Zanger

DIMENSIONS

PATTERNS AND PROFILES COMBINED TO CREATE
UNIQUE DIMENSIONAL DESIGNS IN FLOORING.

What began as a concept in Spring 2006 to take familiar shapes and
patterns provided by other popular flooring materials and make them in
a resilient rubber tile, has become the best innovation the rubber flooring
market has seen in decades. Introducing Roppe Dimensions Rubber Tile.

All patterns are familiar in design, but are now available with the added
benefits that can be found only in rubber flooring prodcts – inherent slip
resistence, comfort under foot, sound deadening qualities, enhanced ROI
in comparison to other flooring options and their required maintenance
procedures.

WITH ROPPE THE POSSIBILITIES ARE ENDLESS.
YOU DESIGN IT AND WE'LL HELP YOU MAKE IT HAPPEN.

ROPPE
Proven. Flooring. Experiences.

 SINGLE

1.800.537.9527 | www.roppe.com

Fabrics: HBF, Knoll, Maharam
Lighting: Artemide, Bartco, Corelite, Delray Lighting, Elliptipar, Focal Point, Itre, Leucos, Lightolier, Litecontrol, Lithonia, Louis Poulsen, Luxo, Pinnacle,
Ceilings: Armstrong, USG
Wallcoverings and Paint: Benjamin Moore, Scuffmaster, Sherwin-Williams, Wolf Gordon
Window Treatments: MechoShade
General Contractors: DPR Construction
Lighting Consultants: NELSON

Financial Services Firm
Design Firm: Ted Moudis Associates
Furniture: Bernhardt, CCN, HBF, Herman Miller, Steelcase, TexStyle
Carpets & Flooring: Bentley Prince Street, Innovative Stone, Interface, Nichols, Stone Source, Tuva Looms
Fabrics: ArcCom, Innovations Textiles, Joseph Noble, Knoll Textiles, Kvadrat, Luna Textiles, Spinneybeck Leather, Tokay Blue
Lighting: Boyd, Custom Metalcraft, D'ac, Lighting Solutions, Lucifer, Philips Solid, Selux, Specialty Lighting, Zumtobel
Ceilings: Armstrong, Decoustics
Wallcoverings and Paint: A&G Marble Importers, ArcCom, Ceasar Ceramics, DalTile, Knoll Textiles, Vitruv
Window Treatments: Phifer Wire Products, Sol-R-Control
General Contractors: Lehr Construction Corporation
Lighting Consultants: Patdo Light Studio

Gibraltar Bank
Design Firm: RTKL Associates
Furniture: A. Rudin Furniture, Baker, David Edward, Decca, Fine Living Furniture, Holly Hunt, J3 Designs, Keilhauer, Krug, Lucien Rollin, Office Specialty, Powell & Bonnell Furniture, Sun Furniture, Touhy
Carpets & Flooring: Invision, Keys Granite, Marmoleum, Old World Flooring
Fabrics: Carnegie, Edelman Leather, HBF, Kravet Fabrics, Lee Jofa, Moore & Giles, Pierre Frey, Rogers & Goffigon, Schumacher, Stroheim & Romann, Zimmer & Rohde
Lighting: Artemide, Beghelli, Fuse Lighting, HE Williams, Infinity, Kramer Lighting, Schmitzer/Inter-Lux, USA Illuminations
Ceilings: Armstrong
Wallcoverings and Paint: Benjamin Moore, Eykon, F. Schumacher & Co., JM Lynn, Koroseal, Maharam

General Contractors: Americon Global Management Consulting Firm
Design Firm: Rottet Studio
Furniture: Brayton, Decca, Sandler, Steelcase
Carpets & Flooring: Constantine, Invision, Scott Group
Fabrics: Bernhardt, Carnegie, Polllack, Spinneybeck Leather
General Contractors: Trademark Construction

Greystar Real Estate Partners
Design Firm: LS3P Associates Ltd.
Furniture: ESD, Knoll, Tekmon
Carpets & Flooring: Charleston One Source, Tandus
Lighting: Artemide, Global, Translite Sonoma, Urban Electric
Wallcoverings and Paint: ICI, Maharam
Window Treatments: Hopes Window Systems, Vimco Shade Systems
General Contractors: Carolina Services

Hacienda Builders
Design Firm: McCarthy Nordburg
Furniture: AIS Systems Furniture, A-Rudin, Martin Brattrud
Carpets & Flooring: Arizona Tile, Cactus Tile, Cambridge Carpet, Invision,
Fabrics: HBF, Joseph Noble
Lighting: Alfa, Kurt Versen, Sistemalux, Winona
Ceilings: Armstrong
Wallcoverings and Paint: Dunn Edwards, Knoll, Maharam, Wolf-Gordon
General Contractors: Opus West Corporation
Lighting Consultants: Arizona Lighting

Haworth Calgary Showroom & Learning Centre
Design Firm: Perkins+Will
Furniture: Haworth
Carpets & Flooring: Bentley Prince Street, Interface, Shaw Commercial
Fabrics: Carnegie, Haworth, Luna, Maharam
Lighting: DoSAL, Elliptipar, Gotham, Linear Lighting
Ceilings: 9Wood, Armstrong
Wallcoverings and Paint: Benjamin Moore, Haworth, Timeless Timber
Window Treatments: Carnegie
General Contractors: Haworth, Inc.
Lighting Consultants: Perkins+Will

Healthcare Administration Company, Headquarters and Service Center
Design Firm: McCarthy Nordburg
Furniture: Carolina, Harter, Martin Brattrud
Carpets & Flooring: Arizona Tile, Crossville, Shaw Contract
Fabrics: Architex, Brentano, HBF Textiles, Maharam, Paul Brayton
Lighting: Bruck Lighting, Gotham, Lithonia
Ceilings: Armstrong
Wallcoverings and Paint: Carnegie, Frazee, Maharam, Maya Romanoff, Sherwin-Williams
Window Treatments: MechoShade
General Contractors: Wespac Construction
Lighting Consultants: RC-Lurie

HLM Venture Partners
Design Firm: Margulies Perruzzi Architects
Furniture: Facility Management Associates
Carpets & Flooring: Shep Brown Associated
Lighting: Reflex Lighting Group
Ceilings: Armstrong
Wallcoverings and Paint: Benjamin Moore, California Paint
Window Treatments: Metco
General Contractors: Jones Lang LaSalle
Lighting Consultants: AJ Dean

Hunter Roberts Interiors
Design Firm: Ted Moudis Associates
Furniture: Bernard, Haworth, Knoll
Carpets & Flooring: Bentley, Invision, Murmo Leun, Tuva
Fabrics: Bernhardt, Carnegie, Elmo Leathers, Holly Hunt, Luna, Spinneybeck Leather
Lighting: Litecontrol, Lucifer, National, Selux, Specialty Lighting, Trans Lite Sonoma, Zumtobel
Ceilings: Armstrong
Wallcoverings and Paint: Benjamin Moore, Knoll
Window Treatments: Sol-R-Shade
General Contractors: Hunter Roberts Interiors

Investment Management Firm
Design Firm: Ted Moudis Associates
Furniture: Baker, Bernhardt, Halcon, Herman Miller, TexStyle
Carpets & Flooring: Bentley, Lonseal, Stone Source, Tuva, Woolshire
Fabrics: Bergamo, Holly Hunt, Luna, Maharam, Sina Pearson, Spinneybeck Leather
Lighting: Concealite, Litecontrol, Lucifer, National, Selux, Specialty Lighting
Ceilings: Armstrong, Decoustics
Wallcoverings and Paint: Benjamin Moore, Innvironments, Maharam, Scuffmaster

General Contractors: Structure Tone
Lighting Consultants: Jason Design Group

Kho + Patel
Design Firm: H. Hendy Associates
Furniture: SWM Construction
Carpets & Flooring: Grasscloth/Chilewich, Shaw Carpet
Lighting: Leucos Lighting, Lumetta
Wallcoverings and Paint: Donghia, Innovative Wallcoverings
Window Treatments: Skyco Roller Shades
General Contractors: Al Lee Development

Kimball Office
Design Firm: Huntsman Architectural Group
Furniture: Kimball
Carpets & Flooring: Bentley Prince Street
Lighting: Architectural Lighting Works, Foscarini
Ceilings: Armstrong
Wallcoverings and Paint: Kelly Moore
General Contractors: GCI

Kushner Companies, New York City Offices
Design Firm: Gerner Kronick + Valcarcel, Architects, PC
Furniture: David Edwards, Knoll, M2L Collections, Matteo Grassi, Viacraft Custom Mill Workers, Walter P. Sauer Custom Furniture Makers, Zographos
Carpets & Flooring: Bentley Prince Street
Fabrics: David Edwards, Matteo Grassi
Lighting: Erco, Zumtobel
Ceilings: Sound Seal
Wallcoverings and Paint: Benjamin Moore, Wolf-Gordon
Lighting Consultants: Jerry Kugler Lighting Design

Liskow & Lewis
Design Firm: Ken R. Harry Associates, Inc.
Furniture: David Edward, Geiger Intl, HBF, Keilhauer, Knoll, Patella
Carpets & Flooring: Masland Contract, National Terrazzo, Tile & Marble
Fabrics: Cortina Leather, Knoll Textiles, Momentum, Pollack
Lighting: Boyd Lighting, Celestial Lighting, Lightolier
Ceilings: Armstrong
Wallcoverings and Paint: Benjamin Moore, Carnegie, Maharam
Window Treatments: Nysan Shade Systems
General Contractors: Spaw Maxwell
Lighting Consultants: Ken R. Harry Associates, Inc.

Logan Circle Partners, L.P.
Design Firm: Partridge Architects Inc.
Furniture: Bernhardt, HBF, ICF, Jofco, Lowenstein, Teknion, Vitra, Woodtronics
Carpets & Flooring: Shaw Contract
Lighting: Prima
General Contractors: Cyma Builders & Construction Managers

A Major Financial Services Company, Boston, Mass.
Design Firm: Margulies Perruzzi Architects
Furniture: Office Solutions
Carpets & Flooring: Armstrong, Interface
Fabrics: ArcCom, Architex, Designtex, HBF, Knoll Textiles, LJH, Maharam, Robert Allen, Spinneybeck
Lighting: Artemide, Boyd Lighting, Del Ray, Leucos, Lightolier, Lithonia, Mark Lighting, Specialty Lighting Industries, Zumtobel
Ceilings: Armstrong, USG
Wallcoverings and Paint: Architex, Benjamin Moore, Carnegie, Innovations, Knoll, Maharam, Wolf-Gordon
General Contractors: Tishman Construction
Lighting Consultants: Lisa Zidel Lighting Design

A Major Insurance Company, Hingham, Mass.
Design Firm: Margulies Perruzzi Architects
Furniture: Corporate Interiors, Office Environments
Carpets & Flooring: Atlas, Interface
Fabrics: Architex
Lighting: Louis Poulsen, Peerless
Ceilings: Armstrong
Wallcoverings and Paint: Benjamin Moore
Window Treatments: MechoShade
General Contractors: Turner Construction Company
Lighting Consultants: Lisa Zidel Lighting Design

Mazama Capital Management
Design Firm: Tobin + Parnes Design Enterprises
Furniture: Antoine Proulx, Bernhardt, Bright, Davis, Dennis Miller, HBF, Herman Miller, Holly Hunt, Knoll, Steelcase, Teknion, Touhy
Carpets & Flooring: Amtico, Atlas Carpet, Pianeto Legno, Tufenkian, Woolshire
Fabrics: Bernhardt Textiles, Designtex, Maharam, Pollack, TexStyle
Lighting: Artemide, Bartco Lighting, Boyd Lighting, Celestial Lighting, Hemera, Specialty Lighting Industries, Linear Lighting, USA Illumination, WaterWorks
Wallcoverings and Paint: Angela Brown, Benjamin Moore, Maharam, Modular Arts, Sanitas, 3Form, Vitruv, Wolf Gordon

MediaCom Offices
Design Firm: HOK Canada
Furniture: Herman Miller
Carpets & Flooring: Interface
Fabrics: Maharam
Lighting: Wesco/Plan Electric
Wallcoverings and Paint: Benjamin Moore
Window Treatments: Solarfective
General Contractors: Marant Construction
Lighting Consultants: Joe Galeazza of TPL Lighting

MediaVest
Design Firm: NELSON
Furniture: Haworth, Herman Miller, Steelcase, Stylex
Carpets & Flooring: ASI Flooring, Bentley Prince Street, Masland Contract
Fabrics: Abet Laminati, ARPA, Bernhardt, Momentum
Lighting: Alix Lighting, Lightolier, Louis Poulsen
Ceilings: Armstrong
Wallcoverings and Paint: Benjamin Moore, Sherwin-Williams, Wolf Gordon
General Contractors: Lehr Construction

Mercedes-Benz of San Francisco
Design Firm: Huntsman Architectural Group
Furniture: Steelcase
Carpets & Flooring: Auto Form, Bentley Prince Street, Forbo, Interface
Lighting: Finelite, Gotham
Ceilings: Armstrong
Wallcoverings and Paint: Kelly Moore, Scuffmaster
General Contractors: Plant Construction Company, L.P.

Microsoft Building 88
Design Firm: Zimmer Gunsul Frasca Architects LLP
Furniture: Davis, d'Tank, Harter, IDX, INDX, ISA, Keilhauer, KI, Urban Hardwoods, Watson
Carpets & Flooring: Interface, Tate Access Floor
Fabrics: HBF Textiles, Knoll, Maharam, Sina Pearson
Ceilings: Armstrong
Wallcoverings and Paint: Benjamin Moore
General Contractors: Seellen Construction
Lighting Consultants: Gerber Engineering

Montgomery & Co.
Design Firm: BraytonHughes Design Studios
Furniture: Academia, Davis, Herman Miller, Martin Brattrud, Meridian, Vitra, Woodtech
Carpets & Flooring: ASN Natural Stone, Invision

HUNTER ROBERTS

For Hunter Roberts, it is about our understanding of the expectations of our clients, partners and the communities we work in.

From preconstruction to completion, we bring financial resources, depth of expertise, accountability and recognized leadership. The result is a common understanding which enables success and the ability to assemble the right team to build enduring relationships.

we listen. we communicate. we deliver.

SERVICES
PRECONSTRUCTION
CONSTRUCTION MANAGEMENT
GENERAL CONTRACTING
CONSULTING
CARPENTRY/FINISH

MARKET SECTORS
CORPORATE INTERIORS
COMMERCIAL
RESIDENTIAL
RETAIL
EDUCATION
HEALTHCARE
PUBLIC SECTOR
SPORTS
PHARMACEUTICALS
HOTELS
DORMITORIES

2 MADISON AVENUE, 2ND FLOOR
W YORK, NY 10016
2.792.0300

VORLD FINANCIAL CENTER, 6TH FLOOR
W YORK, NY 10281
2.321.6800

YORK   NEW JERSEY   PENNSYLVANIA   CONNECTICUT   NORTH CAROLINA

Fabrics: Paul Brayton
Lighting: Artemide, Boyd, De Majo-IE, Focal Point
Ceilings: Armstrong
Wallcoverings and Paint: Benjamin Moore, Scuffmaster
Window Treatments: Designtex

National Gypsum Headquarters Renovations
Design Firm: LS3P Associates Ltd.
Furniture: Aeron, Cambia, Emu Segno, Geiger, Herman Miller, Keilhauer, Nucraft
Lighting: Bega, Bruck, iLight Technologies, Kurt Versen, LBL Lighting, Lithonia
Ceilings: Armstrong
Wallcoverings and Paint: National Gypsum
Window Treatments: MechoShade
General Contractors: R.T. Dooley

Nina Footwear Corporate Headquarters
Design Firm: HOK
Furniture: Alexander Taylor, Knoll, Maria Pergay, Thomas O'Brian
Carpets & Flooring: Allstate, Armstrong, ARPA USA, Daltile, Interface, Johnsonite, Pionite, Roppe
Lighting: Lightolier
Wallcoverings and Paint: Benjamin Moore, Knoll Textiles, Scuffmaster
General Contractors: John Gallin & Son
Lighting Consultants: Mark Architectural Lighting

Nixon Peabody
Design Firm: Gensler
Furniture: Allsteel, Bernhardt, Datesweiser, Gunlocke, Haworth, HBF
Carpets & Flooring: Bentley, Eco-Timber, Forbo
Fabrics: Sina Pearson
Lighting: Kurt Versen
Ceilings: Armstrong
Wallcoverings and Paint: Benjamin Moore, Dunn Edwards, Scuffmaster
Window Treatments: MechoShade
General Contractors: Principal Builders
Lighting Consultants: Studio three twenty one

Nuvera Fuel Cells World Headquarters
Design Firm: Margulies Peruzzi Architects
Furniture: Creative Office Pavilion
Carpets & Flooring: Patcraft
Fabrics: Herman Miller, Knoll
Lighting: Cooper Lighting, Reflex Lighting Group
Ceilings: USG
Wallcoverings and Paint: Benjamin Moore
Window Treatments: Bali Blinds
General Contractors: Erland Construction
Lighting Consultants: Reflex Lighting Group

Partridge Architects Inc.
Design Firm: Partridge Architects Inc.
Furniture: Herman Miller, Knoll, Steelcase
Carpets & Flooring: Shaw Contract
Fabrics: Knoll
Lighting: Delray, Douglas Controls, Gammalux, Lightolier, Pinnacle, Prima
Ceilings: Armstrong
Wallcoverings and Paint: MAB Paints
General Contractors: D'Lauro & Rodgers Inc.

Paul, Hastings, Janofsky and Walker, London
Design Firm: DMJM Rottet / Rottet Studio
Furniture: Holly Hunt, Knoll, Minotti, Vitra
Carpets & Flooring: Karastan
Fabrics: Holly Hunt
Lighting: Cappelini, Selux
Ceilings: Hunter Douglas
Wallcoverings and Paint: John Hutton, Maharam
General Contractors: BW Interiors
Lighting Consultants: Hilson Moran

Paul, Hastings, Janofsky and Walker, Shanghai
Design Firm: Rottet Studio
Furniture: Baker, Bene, Decca Contract, Kokuyo, Steelcase
Carpets & Flooring: Constantine, Odegard, Shaw Contract
Fabrics: Bergamo, Garrett Leather, Jim Thompson, Knoll, Maharam, Rubelli
Lighting: Thorn, Zumtobel
Ceilings: Eurospan
General Contractors: K.R. Architects
Lighting Consultants: HLB

Private Equity Firm
Design Firm: BraytonHughes Design Studios
Furniture: Bernhardt, Knoll, Nienkamper, Vitra, Zographos
Lighting: Kramer, Kurt Versen, Selux
Lighting Consultants: George Sexton & Associates

Reelz Channel
Design Firm: Wolcott Architecture Interiors
Furniture: Allsteel, Westfall Commercial Furniture
Carpets & Flooring: Karastan
Fabrics: Knoll, Maharam
Lighting: Del Ray, Intense, Lithonia
Ceilings: USG
Wallcoverings and Paint: Frazee
Window Treatments: MechoShade
General Contractors: Cal Pae Contractors

Schlumberger Information Solutions - SIS Breakthrough Performance Center
Design Firm: Ken R. Harry Associates, Inc.
Furniture: Allermuir, Humanscale, Leland Intl, OFS, Prismatique
Carpets & Flooring: Monterey, National Terrazzo, Tile & Marble, Inc.
Fabrics: Momentum
Lighting: Lightolier, Litecontrol
Ceilings: Armstrong, Decoustics
Wallcoverings and Paint: Benjamin Moore, Carnegie
Window Treatments: MechoShade
General Contractors: Anslow Bryant Construction
Lighting Consultants: Ken R. Harry Associates, Inc.

Schroders
Design Firm: HLW International LLP
Furniture: B&B Italia, Fritz Hansen, Howe, Vitra, Walter Knoll
Carpets & Flooring: Designtex, Interface, Lees
Fabrics: Kvadrat
Lighting: Modular, Zumtobel
Ceilings: SAS International
Wallcoverings and Paint: Armourcoat, Dulux, Kvadrat
Window Treatments: Architectural Window Films, Verosol, BV
General Contractors: Ibex Interiors, Benbows Interiors, Clestra & Optima
Lighting Consultants: Meit Associates

SJ Berwin
Design Firm: HOK
Furniture: Coexistence, Unifor, Vitra, Wilkhahn
Carpets & Flooring: Altro, Interface
Fabrics: Kvadrat
Lighting: Erco, Whitegoods
Ceilings: SAS International
Wallcoverings and Paint: Dulux
Window Treatments: Claxton Blinds
General Contractors: Overbury
Lighting Consultants: Minds Eye

Skadden Arpa Slate Meagher& Flom LLP
Design Firm: Ken R. Harry Associates, Inc.
Furniture: Bernhardt, HBF, ICI
Carpets & Flooring: Constantine Commercial Carpet, Edward Fields, National Terrazzo, Tile & Marble
Fabrics: Carnegie, HBF, ICF
Lighting: Lightolier, Litecontrol
Ceilings: Armstrong

NeoCon® World's Trade Fair
Chicago
June 15-17, 2009
neocon.com

NeoCon®
World's Trade Fair

IIDEX/NeoCon® Canada
Toronto
September 25–26, 2008
iidexneocon.com

IIDEX
NeoCon Canada

NeoCon® East
Baltimore
October 29–30, 2008
neoconeast.com

NeoCon® East

National Exposition of Contract Furnishings
To exhibit or register to attend, visit merchandisemartproperties.com or call 800.677.6278.

Merchandise Mart
Properties, Inc.

Wallcoverings and Paint: Carnegie, Pratt & Lambert
General Contractors: Spaw Maxwell
Lighting Consultants: Ken R. Harry Associates, Inc.

S. USA Life Insurance
Design Firm: Tobin + Parnes Design Enterprises
Furniture: Bernhardt, Brayton International, Bright, Brueton, Davis, Dennis Miller, Desiron, HBF, M2L, Steelcase, Teknion, Touhy
Carpets & Flooring: Amtico, Armstrong, Atlas Carpet, Bentley, Daltile, Stone Source, Tufenkian
Fabrics: Angela Brown, Architex, Carnegie, Corian, Edelman Leather, Maharam, Pollack, Spinneybeck Leather, Unika Vaev, Walker Zanger,
Lighting: Con-Tech Lighting, Flos USA, LBL Lighting, Lightolier, Lithonia, LuxLuce, Primus Lighting, Quorum International, Studio Italia Design, Translite, USG, WAC Lighting
Ceilings: Armstrong
Wallcoverings and Paint: Abet Laminati, Formica, Lightblocks, Modernfold, Nevamar, Teknion, 3Form, Vitruv
Window Treatments: Sol-R-Shade

TELUS Corporation, TELUS House Atrium
Design Firm: Perkins+Will
Furniture: Keilhauer
Carpets & Flooring: Ceramiche Caesar Porcelain Tile, Interface
Lighting: BPW, Iguzzini Lingotto
Wallcoverings and Paint: Tectum Wall Panels, Telus Graphics
General Contractors: Dominion Construction
Lighting Consultants: Schenke/Bawol Engineering Ltd.

Tobin + Parnes Design Enterprises
Design Firm: Tobin + Parnes Design Enterprises
Furniture: Bernhardt, Davis, Global, Mayline, Neinkamper, Rimadesio, Steelcase
Carpets & Flooring: Allstate, Atlas Carpet, Shaw Contract, Stone Source
Fabrics: Knoll, Maharam
Lighting: Artemide, Cooper, Halo, Lightolier, Luminaire, Metalux, Modem Fan, Nessen, Restoration Hardware, WAC Lighting
Wallcoverings and Paint: Benjamin Moore
Window Treatments: Deko Roller Shading System

The Tower at Lake Carolyn
Design Firm: STAFFELBACH
Furniture: Keilhamer
Carpets & Flooring: Arizona Tile, Horizon Tile

Lighting: Energie, Kurt Versen
Ceilings: Armstrong
Wallcoverings and Paint: Benjamin Moore, Southwest Progressive Enterprises
General Contractors: Scott & Reid General Contractors, Inc.
Lighting Consultants: Lang Lighting Design

University of Arizona, Keating & MRB
Design Firm: Zimmer Gunsul Frasca Architects LLP
Carpets & Flooring: Armstrong, Daltile, Prince Street
Lighting: Edison Price, Lightolier, Louis Poulsen, Paramout, Prudential Lighting, Zumtobel
Ceilings: Armstrong
Wallcoverings and Paint: Frazee, Johnsonite, Sherwin-Williams
Window Treatments: Levolor Contract

University of Oregon Athletic Medicine Center
Design Firm: Zimmer Gunsul Frasca Architects LLP
Furniture: Herman Miller, Mariner Production LLC, Paola Lenti
Carpets & Flooring: Eco-Tile, Scandia
Fabrics: Graybear Leather
Lighting: Culver Glass
Wallcoverings and Paint: Acrylite, Nikolai Manufacturing Inc.

Urban Towers
Design Firm: STAFFELACH
Furniture: Nienkamper
Carpets & Flooring: Burlington Stone, Constantine Commercial Carpet, Stone Marketing International
Lighting: Prescolite
Ceilings: Simplex Ceilings
Wallcoverings and Paint: Benjamin Moore, Southwest Progressive Enterprises
General Contractors: Turner Construction, Metroplex Construction
Lighting Consultants: Lang Lighting Design

Visitor Information Center
Design Firm: McCarthy Nordburg
Furniture: Herman Miller, Lazy Boy, Stylex
Carpets & Flooring: Armstrong, Atlas, Daltile
Lighting: Bruck Lighting, Eureka, Lithonia
Ceilings: Armstrong
Wallcoverings and Paint: Dunn Edwards, Saundra Alexander
General Contractors: Hardison Downey

VW/Audi Design Center
Design Firm: Wolcott Architecture Interiors
Carpets & Flooring: Karastan, Natural Slate, Sureflexx
Lighting: Artemide, Del Ray, Focal Point, Hydrel, Insight, Louis Poulsen, Lutron, Metalux, Zumtobel
Ceilings: Armstrong, Halycon, USG
Wallcoverings and Paint: Frazee, Scuffmaster
Window Treatments: MechoShade
General Contractors: Turelk Construction
Lighting Consultants: PBQA Architectural Lighting

Warren Wixen Real Estate
Design Firm: HLW International LLP
Furniture: Allermuir, Cassina USA, Curtis Varner Furniture & Cabinetry, Fritz Hansen, Source Int'l, Steelcase, Task Chairs
Carpets & Flooring: Constantine Commercial, Solnhofen, Walker Zanger
Fabrics: Designtex, Knoll
Lighting: Base Building Standards, Herman Miller
Ceilings: Halycon
Wallcoverings and Paint: ICI
General Contractors: Howard Building Contractors
Lighting Consultants: HLB Lighting

Winstead PC
Design Firm: Ken R. Harry Associates, Inc.
Furniture: David Edward, Fortress, Halcon, HBF, Martin Brattrud
Carpets & Flooring: National Terrazzo, Tile & Marble, Shaw Contract
Fabrics: Bernhardt, Knoll, Spinneybeck
Lighting: Celestial Lighting, Lightolier, Litecontrol
Ceilings: Armstrong, Decoustics
Wallcoverings and Paint: Benjamin Moore, Carnegie, Knoll
Window Treatments: MechoShade
General Contractors: J.E. Dunn Construction
Lighting Consultants: Ken R. Harry Associates, Inc.

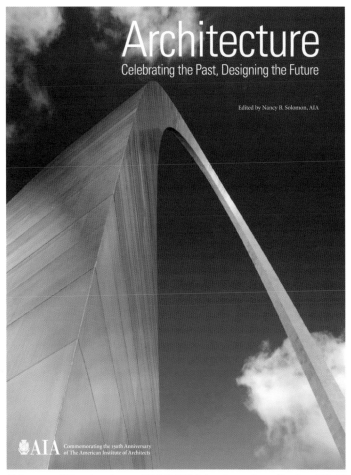

Architecture
Celebrating the Past, Designing the Future

Edited by Nancy B. Solomon, AIA

AIA Commemorating the 150th Anniversary of The American Institute of Architects

424 pages, 560 color photos, 9½" X 12½", hardbound, retail price: $95.00

Commemorating the 150th Anniversary of The American Institute of Architects

This lavishly illustrated book provides a grand tour of the places where we live, work, and play and introduces us to the extraordinary men and women whose ideas are changing the face of communities here and abroad. On the occasion of its 150th anniversary, the American Institute of Architects asked more than 70 contributors to examine the complex and evolving role of America's architects in shaping our cities and communities. Through provocative essays, vignettes, and profiles, illustrated with more than 560 photographs, *Architecture* provides an unprecedented look at the breadth and depth of the architecture profession and points to the significant contributions architects have made in all aspects of society. Most important, the book demonstrates the value of applying "architectural thinking" to the many serious issues—from global warming and homeland security to accessibility and diversity—facing our world today. Practitioners, educators, journalists, and others discuss the historical, philosophical implications. Essays highlight the inspirational work of the recipients of the AIA's highest honor, the Gold Medal, as well as collaborative efforts at the grass-roots level to develop creative strategies for "smart" or "green" growth in communities here and abroad. Contributors include architects Thom Mayne and Robert A.M. Stern, scholar James Steele, journalist Paul Goldberger, and many other leading voices.

Available in bookstores or visit www.visualreference.com

Visual Reference Publications, Inc. 302 Fifth Avenue, New York, NY 10001 (212) 279-7000

contract
inspiring commercial design solutions

PROMOSEDIA
2008 CHAIRS AND MUCH MORE

 search

site | web

home | news | products | design | competitions & awards | industry resources | interact

Contract Magazine Home > *Interior Design Trends*

design

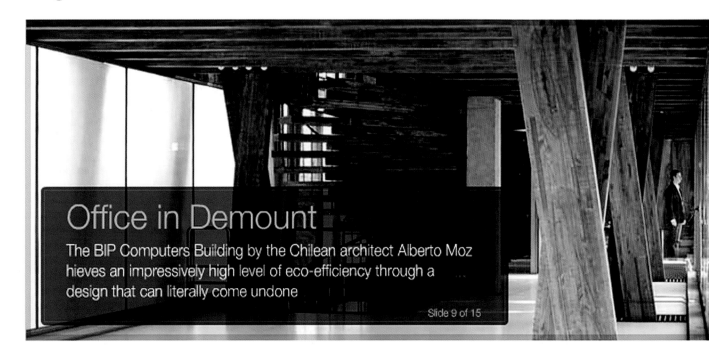

Office in Demount

The BIP Computers Building by the Chilean architect Alberto Moz hieves an impressively high level of eco-efficiency through a design that can literally come undone

Slide 9 of 15

design news

LEED® Gold

Groundbreaking Ceremonies Held for Utah Museum of Natural History

New site to achieve

Southern Land Company Sweetens Up

features

Re-Soled

○ More Corporate Design

Lofty Ideals

○ More Retail Design

adver

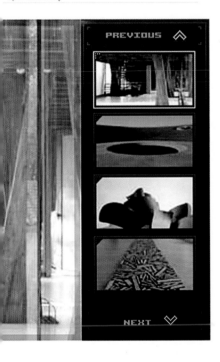

inspiring commercial design

For almost 50 years, *Contract* has been the trusted source of commercial design knowledge, connecting professionals, processes, products, and projects. *Contract* elevates the relevance and value of commercial design by focusing on its power to transform business environments. Through in-depth exploration of the design process, *Contract* delivers the content and context design professionals need to apply smart, real-world solutions in their own practices.

On our Web site you will find:

• the latest product trends and information

• portal to submit projects and products

• information about awards programs and industry events

• our latest design stories

Not a *Contract* subscriber yet?
Go to **www.contractmagazine.com/subscribe**
Or you can enjoy *Contract* for free by viewing our magazine online at **www.contractconnected.com**

Contract is the **only** publication solely devoted to the commercial design profession.

contract

inspiring commercial design solutions

Daylighting, efficient design, color, and community leadership are among the many factors that lead to a successful and sustainable design. AIA Architects stand ready to help ensure a healthy future for us all.

The next step is **up to you.**

By providing the integrated and sustainable design solutions that modern health systems demand, an AIA Architect can help you take the next step toward sustainability and patient well-being.

Walk the Walk
Architects Leading the Sustainable Evolution^{SM}

THE AMERICAN INSTITUTE OF ARCHITECTS

Join us and together we can walk toward a more sustainable future.
Visit **www.aia.org/walkthewalk** today.

The Designer Series

Visual Reference Publications, Inc.
302 Fifth Avenue, New York, NY 10001
212.279.7000 • Fax 212.279.7014
www.visualreference.com

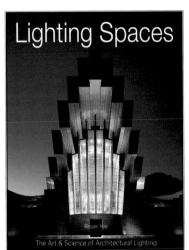

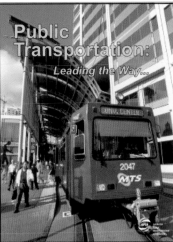

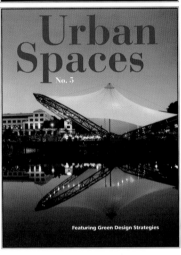

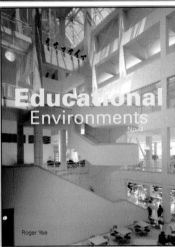

Advertiser Index

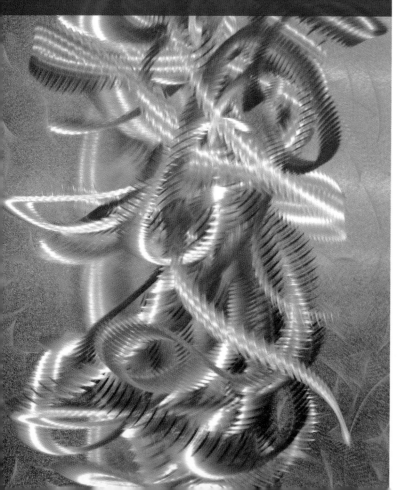

Index by Project